ENDORSEMENTS

This book will challenge your presuppositions, correct your false thinking, and guide you into an intimate relationship with Jesus Christ. This seasoned counselor and ministry leader, with the skill of a surgeon, probes, and cuts away at the malady of your heart, enabling you to experience God's healing grace.

Southern Baptist Pastor

I listened with my heart to the Abbot's straight forward way of exposing the basic truth about how to trust God. I felt a relief at learning the lies we believe about our Lord. The book points out the myths and roadblocks we all create to hinder the path to a life well lived. He has the reader go on a clear and honest pilgrimage to build a relationship with God, a relationship that makes a difference.

Catholic, the Center Coordinator and Assistant Program Director for St. Placid Priory's Spirituality Center

While reading *Listen with the Ear of Your Heart* I found areas I need to trust God more. I loved the analogy of God giving us one mouth and two ears speak less and listen more. We need to remember to give Him the time of listening. This book is an excellent way of helping myself and others to do just that.

Moravian, Single Mother, Optician

This book is for every Christian who seeks an honest and intimate relationship with God. Drawn from decades of experience in education, ministry, and counseling, the Abbot gives readers the tools required to remove the obstacles to a spiritual union with God. This is a transformational work.

Cistercian monk/priest

God provides opportunities to deepen our relationships with Him throughout our lives. This book offers you just such an opportunity. The book is short and to the point, and there is a solid depth to the writing. The author speaks with a wisdom gained through much experience in helping others on their spiritual pilgrimage.

Anglican Bishop

Abbot Oscar Joseph takes you on an amazing journey of discovering the trust and intimacy that you can have in a loving and compassionate God. The Abbot exposes subtle lies that eventually erode your foundational trust in God. He then walks you through your pilgrimage to true intimacy.

Assemblies of God, Mother of 3,
Volunteer Administrative Director

I frequently ask myself, "Is what I am doing effective?" If you are seeking to have a more effective life, you will find Abbot Oscar Joseph's book to be most helpful.

Christian Counselor

When reading through the stories in this book I am reminded that each one of us is on a unique journey, not by ourselves, but with our Creator. It's not about living a perfect life but living it day by day with a God whose grace can redeem us from any mistake or sorrow, can bring us back to life and can restore us to beauty again.

Independent Contemporary Church,
Single Mother, Teaching Assistant

We are so grateful for the wisdom, knowledge, inspiration and guidance that the Abbot provides for this journey which leads by God's grace and forgiveness, to an ultimate destination of personal growth, peace and eternal life.

Methodist, Husband, Professional Fitness Trainer,
Wife, Physician Assistant

Listen with the Ear of Your Heart develops the pilgrim into a better listener consequently able to grow in trust toward God. So like Joseph and Mary, graced by God, we may be able to go beyond what we thought was hardly possible.

Methodist, Medical Professional

LISTEN WITH THE EAR OF YOUR HEART

**Your Pilgrimage
Toward Intimacy
With God**

Abbot Oscar Joseph, O.C.C.O.

Contemplative Monk

Copyright © 2020 Abbot Oscar Joseph, O.C.C.O.

Paperback ISBN: 978-1-64719-045-3
Hardcover ISBN: 978-1-64719-046-0
Epub ISBN: 978-1-64719-047-7
Mobi ISBN: 978-1-64719-048-4

Library of Congress Cataloging in Publication Data
Joseph, O.C.C.O., Abbot Oscar
LISTEN WITH THE EAR OF YOUR HEART: Your Pilgrimage Toward Intimacy with God by Abbot Oscar Joseph, O.C.C.O.
Library of Congress Control Number: 2020920756

Published by BookLocker.com, Inc., St. Petersburg, Florida.

Printed on acid-free paper.

BookLocker.com, Inc.
2020

DEDICATIONS

This Heritage Book is dedicated to my loving daughters;
Michelle, Jennifer and Heather.

CONTENTS

ACKNOWLEDGEMENTS

It becomes easy to acknowledge gratitude when so many people have contributed to the writing of *Listen with the Ear of Your Heart* and those both living and dead who have contributed to the making of myself.

Kathleen, the co-author of my life, makes everything happen. She inspires me to experience more love than I ever thought possible.

Jay Van Nostrand and Rt. Rev. Richard Best are dear friends and editors extraordinaire.

There are many who helped in the "making of myself." I particularly remember those who pushed me to be better and those who held me up at my worst.

Other makers and dear friends are: Primate Rt. Rev. Peter Goodrich, Dr. Dale Hancock, Lance Key, Dr. Jason Crandell, Drs. Arno, and Rev. Sherman McElwain.

The monks and oblates of the Cistercian Order of the Holy Cross fill me with joy and personal fulfillment.

Joyful Julie provided an opportunity for both of us to meet God in profound ways.

Those who are now celebrating the joys of heaven are: my parents, Oscar Joseph and Veronica, Uncles Conrad and Rodger, Mr. Lynch, Father Phillip McKenna, S.J., Bishop Perry Ruby, and precious Jean Heremza.

I also want to thank each of my readers who are seeking a sacred pilgrimage. Blessing to each of you.

PREFACE

by

Abbot Oscar Joseph, O.C.C.O.

Late Friday afternoon, we received a call that my father was about to die. Kathleen, my wife, and I drove through the night from Winston Salem, North Carolina, to Sarasota, Florida. The darkness of the night enveloped me. It was the longest ten hours of my life.

My father was semi comatose. Mom; my sister, Karen; and her adult children were there. I spoke loudly into my father's ear that I, Michael, and Kathleen were there. My soul still wrenches when I think of that moment. I gave him the Church's last rites. I removed his oxygen mask, opened his mouth and gave him Viaticum food for the journey. Shortly after, he died in my arms. It was as though he was waiting for me.

Later when I poured his ashes into his grave, the wind blew and I breathed them in. That was a profound moment of communion with my father I will never forget it.

Dad led a powerful life of hard work, commitment toward excellence and strong faith. That was part of the heritage that he passed on to me. Years later, I took his name during my monastic vows.

At this writing, I am seventy-three and wish to pass my heritage on to you the reader. I have counseled thousands. God has answered my healing prayers for hundreds. I have taught numberless seminars and provided many healing services. I have not only experienced the brokenness of mankind including my own but have also witnessed the human and Divine strength to overcome. I have seen God's grace at the most impossible of times. I wish to pass that on to you.

I firmly believe that no matter where you are or how great or lowly your life may be that our Gracious Lord is pursuing you. He will not let you go. He wants to have an intimate relationship with you. It is my hope that I can teach you as I have thousands of others the truth of God's mercy and love.

Dad's favorite message to me was "Get your education. No one can take that away from you." That inspired me to gain fifty years of advanced academic studies that included doctoral degrees in Christian Counseling and Holy Scripture; forty years of contemplative prayer; thirty-five years of professional Christian Counseling and Spiritual Direction ministry; thirty years celebrating a devout Christian marriage and ordained an Anglican priest, later a bishop; twenty years serving as the Abbot General for the Cistercian Order of the Holy Cross and President of Saint Stephen Harding Theological College and Seminary.

The seeds of my monastic interest were sown in my early teens. I would seclude myself and read books on spirituality. Twenty-three years ago, I took Cistercian monastic vows.

- CHAPTER 1-
PILGRIMAGE

Lord of heaven and earth, may these words be your words.

I am writing from what I know of God, His graciousness, His perpetual love and His incomprehensibility.

He has, over the years, been with me at my most troubled times and my most victorious times. During the troubled times I had abandoned Him. During the most victorious times I had abandoned myself.

Our Good Lord is always with you. You do not need to have more of God because He is already there. What you need is to recognize His presence right here right now.

That is why I am writing these words that I might illustrate His abiding love for you.

God has made you body, soul and spirit. You were made to be drawn to Him, your Creator. God pursues you regardless of your lack of interest in Him and despite your delusional efforts to run toward the satisfaction of what you believe are your true needs. Putting trust in things that rot will get you nowhere. Have you noticed that when you are in real trouble and seek comfort, power, direction and inspiration, you go to the unknown, to the mystical?

You know that you need a close relationship with your merciful Lord. It is only He who can answer your fundamental questions. Where did you come from? Who are you really? Where are you going in your life? How are you going to get there? And when this earthly life is over, what happens to you?

I have counseled hundreds of people with hundreds of problems, hurts, fears and anxieties. But all of them are essentially asking one question, "What is God's will for me?" For them, as for you, that is the question, "What is God's will for me?"

We, you, all of us suffer the universal fears of abandonment and annihilation. Or put in simpler terms, fear of rejection and fear of death. It is easy to understand the fear of rejection. You might even do things out of character to win the approval of others. You might assume the personality or characteristics that your family, culture, employers and churches dictate are the most acceptable. Perhaps you have falsely believed that by having the right job, position, material wealth and superior intellect, you would be loved and accepted.

So you put in an enormous amount of energy and time into acquiring these things that rot. One day, you may realize that a lifetime of misplaced effort was wasted. No matter what you achieved or parts you played, you could never be good enough. You never felt safe to live honestly. You have become more like the walking dead.

God is the real solution. When you know Him well, then you will begin to measure your personal worth not by how others judge you but by how God judges you. When God looks upon you, He sees who you really are. He also sees His Son and the Holy Spirit living within you. When God sees and judges you, He dances.

It can be difficult to imagine that God is pleased with you when you are burdened by the lies of your family, culture, employers and churches. Those lies are simply that, lies.

Your personal sins speak "yes but" deep in your soul. That is indeed another reason to know God. When you know Him, you will also know that He is eager to forgive even your really big sins that you don't want to talk about. "How can that be?" you ask. Simply put, it can be because God said that all you need to do is ask. Carry with you at least a seed of remorse, willingness to reform and lead a better, happier life with His help.

How can you dare embrace God in any way when you do not trust Him? That is the central issue. You do not trust God.

Often the first persons who taught you not to trust were your childhood principal care givers. You accepted their beliefs, hopes and fears. If your principal care givers were not trustworthy, or if they believed that you were not trustworthy, you entered into the swamp of lack of trust. Your childhood first god was your father. If he was not trustworthy but was mean, emotionally distant or even absent, then you start believing that God is not trustworthy, will be judgmental and will not be there for you when you need Him.

And so you grew up in a world that was not safe. You were often suspicious of yourself and others. Naturally, you would build emotional walls against being truly transparent. Those same walls that protected you also hindered you from transparently approaching God. Even if you grew up in the church, it was easy to hide behind the mask of acceptable behaviors and fancy church words. If you did it well, you might have a chance of being accepted. Consequently you have become untrustworthy.

Our culture also teaches you not to trust. Civil laws are basically an effort to give you at least some freedom and security. The law gives you a chance to get what you want if others have a chance to get what they want. Thus we are all equal under the law. Once again, you are trusting things that rot.

The insurance policy on your home is a vehicle that you spend a lot of your time and money to sustain, trusting that it will take care of you should something terrible happen. Many of the policies' clauses list exclusions. Often one of them is called Acts of God. God is described as a threat that you cannot escape. Even the church teaches false pieties and pop psychology through teachings like: "God will never give you more troubles than you can handle." "God is testing you." "God has given you these troubling circumstances so you can get closer to Him." All these statements are false. They describe God as a trickster who plays with His people. They hold you back from trusting God.

In summary, you want to know the important fundamental question. What is the will of God? You want to be safe, accepted and loved by God and others. I have given a brief look at what holds you back from obtaining your needs because fundamentally you trust things that rot.

An intimate relationship with God is your only solution. In that relationship, you will begin to see how lovingly He looks upon you, His creation. God has created you to be drawn to Him. You are able to understand that God is already with you. You can learn that you are already walking in, with and through Him. You can feel accepted and safe. You can lead an authentically inspired life.

Before you begin your pilgrimage, let me say that I do sincerely hope that what I am teaching inspires you. Everything that I teach is always supported by Holy Scripture and the teachings of the Universal Church.

Recently, we had one of our monks travel a total of six thousand miles to visit with us at the Holy Cross Monastery. That was indeed a pilgrimage. She was hoping to be inspired and taught more about her spiritual craft. She wanted to be more aware of God's presence in her life. She wanted a life that was always walking in, with and through God. God did grace her on this pilgrimage. Her pilgrimage was through travel from one place to another.

There is another kind of pilgrimage. In my twenties, I was an egocentric pseudo-intellectual. Now some fifty years later, I am indeed a different person. When I completed my first doctoral requirements, I was filled with anxiety. I realized that I knew nothing. So of course, I went after my second doctorate. That one was in Scripture. When I completed those requirements, I was again full of anxiety because I once again knew that I knew nothing. When I attempted to get a third doctorate, Kathleen, my wife, said, "*Stop, get on with living God's life.*" I then grew in the knowledge that I don't have to know everything. What I also learned is that I could rely on God. After all, He knew everything. Putting my trust in my own intellect and other things that rot got me nowhere.

Years later, a fellow monk and I went white water kayaking.

We were promised instruction before we began but got none. Fortunately, I previously had gotten some instruction from YouTube.

So here we were, foolishly kayaking over white water rapids. The other monk was repeatedly saying the Jesus prayer. I was constantly yelling over the roar of the river, "Help me, God!" We wanted to stay alive and not tip over and lose our kayaks.

After a while, I felt like an expert. Then there they were, right in front of me, many giant rapids. I approached them with the wisdom of You Tube and got caught in the rocks. I knew that if I did not successfully get over these rocks, the nearby rapids would topple me over for sure. So once again, I accessed my vast YouTube knowledge. Nothing worked. I screamed loudly so God could hear me. I said, "God, please teach me something I don't already know." Clear as a bell over the roar of the river, God said, "Put your paddle in the water and don't move it." That seemed strange, but I did it anyways. Immediately, I felt the enormous power of the river against the paddle. The next time I was aware of myself, I was not only successfully over those rocks but also safely beyond the other rapids that had previously threatened me.

That is a great true story. In my desperation, I had to get over myself and listen. That is going to be the first step in your pilgrimage. Get over yourself and just listen.

My wife and I took years of investigation to find the perfect property for the Holy Cross Monastery which was also going to be our home. We had a wishful criterion of trees in a developed neighborhood and a lake. All this had to be close to the center of Winston-Salem, North Carolina. We were asking for a lot.

We looked prayed and looked some more. One day we were exploring, and behold, there it was a tree-filled lot on a lake in a developed neighborhood. Naturally, we ventured forth and found the "For Sale" sign buried under the leaves. We called the owner, got the price and put in a bid. We were in a bidding war with another family.

Previously, God told Kathleen that we would have the property in eighteen months. So here we were on the eighteenth month in a bidding war. Kathleen had previously told God that she wished for the property. God in return said that she had not yet directly asked for it. At which moment she said, "Please, God, give us the property." That afternoon, we won the bidding war and were granted the property. Kathleen later asked God why He had given it to us. God replied, "Because she had trusted Him." And that is a true story.

The first step is to get over yourself. The second step is to grow in trusting our Lord. How are you going to trust when it is not in your sinful nature to do so?

The pilgrimage toward trust is going to be much like ours in preparing to build God's monastery. First, we prayed. Then we consulted Holy Scripture, our reliable guide, for building instructions.

Simply stated, Scripture is reliable truth on faith and morals. It describes the salvation pilgrimage of God's people and His communicating relationship with them.

Your pilgrimage toward trusting in the Lord is a lifelong journey. Your efforts in trusting God are about your pilgrimage toward spiritual and emotional maturity.

Following Scripture and the teachings of the Church Universal, you can clear the trees and get rid of the rocks and other debris. You can pull out the tangled roots deep below the earth. Then you would be ready to lay a foundation and pour the concrete. Having built according to the architect's plan, you can begin to till the soil.

The monastery's contractor said that a project of this size will have some mistakes, something will go wrong. But not to worry, everything can be fixed. That was great advice and gave us a lot of comfort. I actually did look for things that might go wrong with my daily and sometimes hourly inspections. It is that same attention that you have to give toward your pilgrimage. Constantly keep alert, and when troubles occur, confess them. When something went wrong I was quick to point it out. The contractor was great. Never did he defend himself or his laborers. He accepted the fault and immediately not only corrected the fault but also made the solution even better than the original plan.

God will not only forgive your sins but He will also guide you back on to a better course than you could have imagined. Remember, "Where there is sin grace abounds more."

This will be your exciting journey. It will be much like building your inner self. With God's grace, you will get over yourself so that you can clear trees, remove the rocks and debris. You will pull out those tangled roots hidden deep below. Then you will be ready to lay a foundation and pour the concrete. Having begun according to the architect's plan, you can begin to till the soil. This pilgrimage can be challenging. God will help you. Remember, all that you do is already in, with and through Him.

Chapter 1
Pilgrimage
REFLECTIONS

A major theme of this book is establishing a trusting relationship with God. A difficulty in establishing such a relationship is your lack of trust in Him. Your lack of trust is a product of others erroneous beliefs and your own misconceptions based on their and your inability to trust. I will include a reflection on trust. These reflections and others will help you to better understand yourself thus preparing you to enter a deeper more intimate relationship with your Creator.

What do I know about me? Where did I come from? What is my developmental background? Were my parents emotionally available? As a child, did I feel accepted?

Reflections on this chapter:

- Reread the chapter carefully.
- List what you believe are the main points. Which points trouble you the most?
- Why are they troubling?
- How have you addressed these troubling problems in the past?
- What can you do today to resolve these troubling problems?
- You may have had other thoughts not included in this chapter that you should address. What are they?
- How will you resolve them today?
- Write your own personal prayer to God regarding the above information.

- CHAPTER 2 -
FUNDAMENTAL STEPS IN DEVELOPING TRUST

I remember a story about a newspaper reporter interviewing a very holy female mystic. The reporter's first inquiry to the mystic was, "Tell me about God." After a short reflection, the mystic answered, "What can I say about God?" I think of that story often particularly when I encounter God while praying for others. There is no way to describe the experience. Groping for words ends up missing the description all together.

Years ago, I had prayed and counseled with a young emotionally battered woman whose spirit was actually slumbering. Effectively, her spirit was asleep. She was not clinically depressed. She was no longer able to neither connect spiritually nor emotionally with anyone or anything not even herself. No matter how hard she tried, her prayer life was empty. We prayed together for many hours over a period of several weeks. Slowly, her spirit awakened. She was then able to change her life. I cannot begin to describe the wonder I had experienced with the Holy Spirit during those prayer times.

Trying to describe God and the experiences of Him is nearly impossible. The best anyone can do is to speak in metaphors. Metaphors are nice, but they are not always understandable. You want a God whom you can understand. Consequently, you make God into your own image and likeness. That image and likeness is broken and frail.

Let me illustrate from a contemporary example, but let us remember that this illustration could just as easily be Adam and Eve after the fall. I have spent over twenty thousand hours counseling broken and frail people. The broken and frail are dying in their fight or flight. They are full of anxiety. Their hearts are bleeding. They have been rejected by the one who most of all should have accepted them. They are drowning in a pool of destructive emotions. They are broken and frail.

With tears, their words break out. "I did love you. Now I hate you." "You are never there for me." "You are distant from me."

"You do not care."

"You are always too busy." "I don't understand."

"I try but you never seem to care."

"You are always testing me to see if I love you." "I feel unworthy."

In tears, they crumble and give up.

You have used these very same words to describe God. God seems distant, He is too busy to hear your prayers and He seems fickle. He tests you. He seems far away and not interested. You make God like yourself, broken and frail. No wonder you do not trust God. You want to trust Him but you don't. You have to grow in trust. It is not easy.

The first step in pulling out your "tangled roots" is to know that Jesus knows your pilgrimage. Jesus understands our suffering, pain, confusion and loneliness. He, too, was abandoned by traitors.

Take a moment and imagine Jesus on the cross. Jesus can hardly breathe. His blood is pouring out. He is ridiculed. Only a small handful of supporters are with Him. His so-called friends are hiding, gutless wonders.

Look at that picture. Hold it in your mind. Jesus, a God/man, lived much of His life with a single parent and, perhaps, received "welfare funds" from the synagogue. He was frequently ridiculed as the illegitimate son of a loose woman. Jesus hung naked on the cross in front of His mother. He was totally shamed and sexually abused. Even while enduring unbelievable pain, He said, "Forgive them, Father, they know not what they do." His mission now over, He said, "It is finished."

I hope that you will never forget that image of real love. Father God showed His love for you through the obedience of His Son. God knew that you would need such a sacrificial love. While you are grateful for this dynamic expression of God's love, you hardly feel worthy of such an expression. You can walk out of your unworthiness when you realize that you cannot on your own be worthy of anything. God has made you worthy. You will grow more in that wisdom as you relate more intimately with your loving merciful God.

An important part of your pilgrimage is to be aware of who you are at this very moment. The first step toward growing in worthiness and, consequently, trust is to associate with people whom you respect, not vampires. Vampires are those who want to get everything they can from you. They are always doing "poor baby me" manipulative tactics. They are the naysayers, always complaining about something. They never take responsibility for their own situation. Perhaps they even blame God for their misery. These people do not respect you. They are sucking your blood and distracting you from your pilgrimage toward God. Say goodbye to them.

Those that you respect will see you as valuable. They will listen to your story and encourage you. A good example of someone whom I respect is my best friend Dale. He is a Christian counselor and a man of sincere faith. We come from two very different faith traditions. When I use liturgical, ecclesiastic references, he is not always sure what I am saying. But Dale loves me. He listens, in an encouraging way. I always walk away knowing that he loves me. That is what those who respect you will do for you. They may not always understand you and some of your oddly unique behaviors but they will always love you.

Hopefully, some of your trusted people are from a Christian background and belong to a Christian, praying, Bible believing, faith of the Fathers type of church. You need to join such a church. Remember, Jesus built His Church upon the apostles, knowing that you would need constant encouragement, authoritative teaching and be surrounded by loving people who would help you grow in trust and inspire godly behavior toward yourself and others.

Your attitude toward the value of church is vitally important. You can experience God in a wide variety of places but none as vitally unique as participating in a faith community. If you find yourself complaining about Sunday worship, the preaching, choir, seating and the person sitting next to you, something is wrong with you. Perhaps you picked the church for the wrong reasons. Typically people choose a church because it is less than seven stoplights from their home, good programs for children, they like the pastor, music, entertainment, the social hour or their parents went there. These are all the wrong reasons.

Your best approach is to do some research on the church regarding their beliefs. Is the church faithful to the teachings of Scripture and the Church Fathers? Are the Church and the pastor under the supervision of a higher authority? Is the pastor formally educated? Who originally founded that church? You need to put a lot of time and effort into picking a church. It is an awesome responsibility. Remember that the purpose of many churches is to form you into their particular mission. Is that mission what you really want?

You may also complain about your church because you bring nothing to the Sunday service. You might believe, perhaps unspoken, that the Sunday service is your weekly gas station meant for your weekly fill-up. Sunday service is not meant to gas you up. It is a sacred moment when the faithful come together to experience what they cannot experience alone. Sunday service is the experience of God's people coming together for worship, praise, thanksgiving and to encounter a loving and merciful God who is uniquely present to them as a congregation. The sermon was never meant to be your only weekly spiritual inspiration. If you come to the Sunday service without already having been filled with personal and family prayer, the weekly gas station will be closed.

Imagine if your home operated like a domestic church where you pray together with your wife and family who also participate in a local mission. When my children were little, doing their preschool morning rituals, I positioned myself right in the middle of the house so that they could see me praying. At that time, our whole family was working with the local poor. And yes, we were active church members. The children are all grown up with their own families doing similar activities. Our domestic church and the trusted example of their father were passed on to their own children. If you want to witness a trustworthy God at home do the following. It will change your life.

I often teach how to bless your mates and even family members before going off to work. It is simple. The husband begins, the wife approaches her husband, bows her head to receive his blessing. The husband places his hand upon her head. The blessing can be simple, "God, thank you for the gift of this wonderful woman, bless her, keep her safe today, and always in your will and in your peace." The wife then places her hands on his chest and says a prayer somewhat similar. St. Benedict says that prayers should be short and simple. This simple blessing will greatly bless you, your mate and family.

Praying with your mate is not simply a ritual but an act of unity and love toward each other and God. A good example was the occasion when a minister and his wife walked into my counseling room. I noticed that she was limping because of pain in her knee. I asked if he had prayed for her. He had not. I asked him to get on his knees in front of her and pray. He said a ritualistic prayer full of expletives, fancy phrases, rather loudly but unattached and lacking in love for his wife. After the prayer, I asked her how her knee felt, and she replied that it still hurt. I then showed him how to pray as an act of unity with his wife. He prayed sincerely and with fewer words. The wife's knee pain went away. You need not be fancy with your prayers. Pray briefly with love.

If you are to learn about trust, you have to be trustworthy.

You have been influenced by your father's poor representation of God. You can change by better representing God in your own home. If your father was an excellent Christian, then you can honor him by modeling after him. Even if you do not fully trust God, it does not mean that you can sit on the sidelines. You can learn by participation.

The father is the central figure of the home. What the father determines and shows is most important to him will determine what the children later as adults will determine as what is important. God has graced the man to be the spiritual leader, the one who goes first, who makes things happen. All too often the husband leaves a vacuum in the home by hiding out from his responsibilities. This often takes the form of going to pornography, staying unnecessarily long hours at work or some other unnecessary activity. The wife has to fill in.

That is a terrible situation. Wives, I encourage you to speak up and, if necessary, hold your husband's hand and lead him until he is able to walk on his own. That makes you trustworthy and reliable.

I do grieve for and respect those women who, for whatever reason, have to go it alone. It is difficult indeed. Ladies, you can use this as an opportunity to be trustworthy by participating in your extended family and local church.

To summarize, your growth in trusting your Good and Gracious Lord is to remove yourself from the vampires, gather around those whom you respect, join a faithful Christian community, be involved with some ministry, pray at home privately, and with your family. Always have that reliable source, the Holy Bible, before you. I would suggest that you focus on the New Testament and the Letters. There is nothing wrong with the Old Testament, but for the beginner, the New Testament would be better. Let us learn first about the life and Way of Jesus and in the letters about the Way of the Church and right living. Then go to the Old Testament and learn how God brought His people to the moment of the Nativity.

CHAPTER 2
FUNDAMENTAL STEPS IN DEVELOPING TRUST
REFLECTIONS

A major theme of this book is establishing a trusting, intimate relationship with God. A difficulty in establishing such a relationship is your lack of trust in Him. Your lack of trust is a product of others' erroneous beliefs and your own misconceptions based on theirs' and your own inability to trust. I will include a reflection on trust. These reflections and others will help you to better understand yourself, thus preparing you to enter a deeper, more intimate relationship with your Creator.

Although I speak all the right words about Jesus and my relationship with Him, I do not really trust Him. I avoid His lordship over my life. I have to be in charge of my life.

Reflections on this chapter:

- Reread the chapter carefully.
- List what you believe are the main points. Which points trouble you the most?
- Why are they troubling?
- How have you addressed these troubling problems in the past?
- What can you do today to resolve these troubling problems?
- You may have had other thoughts not included in this chapter that you should address. What are they?
- How will you resolve them today?
- Write your own personal prayer to God regarding the above information.

- CHAPTER 3 -
LIES THAT YOUR MAMA AND EVERYONE ELSE TOLD YOU

Yes, lies told to you by everyone. I hear these lies every day. Social media is loaded with religious lies. The lies appear to be truthful, comforting and are easily digested. They appeal to your broken, frail self.

I can't stand the lies because they draw the wrong picture of God and Christianity. These lies hurt people. Often the liar doesn't even know they are lies. When I see them on Facebook, I usually try to correct the individual who posted them. About99.8 percent of the time, the poster and their friends just argue back. Ignorance reigns. People are resistant to truth. Fortunately, the more you know and trust God, the more you will intuitively recognize lies as not representing the true character of God.

The root of most lies is to recreate Scripture to be a book of magic answers. For example, a troubled person looks for the magic answer, opens the book to a random pageant reads a random quote. The quote is a description of Judas hanging himself. The person now opens to another random page and reads another random quote that says, "And do likewise." Scripture is reliable, but it was not meant to be magical.

You might have a specific problem and go to Scripture for a specific answer. You might start by going to the glossary to find the name of your problem. You soon learn that in utero fertilization is not there. So you falsely conclude that since the reliable book doesn't specifically discuss in utero fertilization, you are at liberty to do whatever you want. Similarly, you are not likely to find the word masturbation in the glossary. So you conclude that you can do whatever you want.

Actually, Scripture has a great deal to say about faith and morals. Sometimes you have to put together several selections of Scripture to get your answer. While there is no direct reference in the New Testament to masturbation, there is a great deal said about selfishness, lust and sexual acts belonging to marriage. Study those areas and you will get your answer on masturbation.

Religious euphemisms are often filled with lies and trickery that reinforce the lie that God is not to be trusted. For example, a family loses an infant to death. A terrible experience to be sure. In an effort to comfort themselves, they say, "God must have needed another angel in heaven. So He took our little baby." My heart certainly goes out to this grieving mother, but look at what is actually being said. God has needs so He brutally takes your helpless baby. In an effort to placate your grief, God makes your baby an angel hoping that you would not notice that your baby now has a lower status in heaven. God is happy and that is all that counts. Can you trust a God who needs His creation in such a way that He plays dirty tricks on them? Such euphemisms generally distract you from the real problem.

What is the cause of infant deaths? America has the highest infant mortality rate of all the developed countries. Wouldn't it be more grief healing to bring a real solution to the problem rather than tagging God as the evil one?

Another lie, "God will not give you any more than you can handle." Here you go again, blaming God for giving you what is really the product of your sowing and reaping. The actual Scriptural reference is "God can overcome any sinful thought that you might have." The euphemism is entirely different than the truth. The truth is much more helpful since your sinful sowing and reaping begins with a sinful thought. If you allow God, He could conquer the sinful thought, thus preventing further sin and its consequences. The lie actually prevents you from a relationship with a loving God who wants the best for you.

A very harmful lie is that God tests you so that you will grow in faith. Let's say it another way. God brings difficulties upon you purposefully so that you will grow in faith. Run from that God. He is not trustworthy. For example, a drunken alcoholic drives recklessly and kills an infant. God tested both the drunk and the family of the infant.

Let me make it very clear. God does not test. However, if you allow God, He can use a situation that you or someone else brought upon you to draw you closer to Him, but He did not cause the situation. If you put these pious euphemisms together, you have created a serious problem. Blaming God for your difficulties rather than taking rightful responsibility, you have reinforced that you are indeed broken and fragile and God is not trustworthy.

The best lies are subtle and are wrapped in some truth. For example: a widely accepted truth is that Sunday is the Lord's Day. "This is the day that the Lord has made. Let us rejoice and be glad." Sunday belongs to God, and you are to worship Him particularly as a group on that holy day. The Day is about God, not you.

A Christian greeting card company morphs "God's day" into "This nice day brings rain of blessings for you. God will take care of you and will strengthen you. Trust in His love. He wants you to do well and be greatly prospered." They turn God's day into our day, all about what we get.

Worship services are not times for evangelization, altar calls, anointing or coming forward for personal prayer. Do all that before or after the service or at another time. Remember, Sunday is the Lord's Day, not ours. Sunday school classes are excellent opportunities to do these wonderfully personal things.

Pop psychology has infiltrated many churches with a feel good philosophy. This example is the one I hate the most because it has destroyed many good people. "You must forgive yourself." A little aside, in Scripture, our reliable source, any time me, my, mine, self, etc. is used, trouble soon follows. Pop psychology is really saying: "Thanks, God, I am so humbled that You have forgiven me. My next step to complete Your forgiveness is for me to forgive myself. It is necessary for me to complete Your forgiveness because something is lacking in Your forgiveness. Fortunately, for me, I can handle Your lack by forgiving myself. I am so happy that by doing so, I become greater than You." Humanism has become a theology.

Lies often make their way into our lives by manipulating the truth or historical accuracy thus misrepresenting God. For example: "When two or three are gathered together, God will be there and He will grant their petitions." About forty years ago, I was in direct sales. Our manager, in a misguided effort to inspire us, would say, "I want sales today. Who else wants sales today?" We would all cheer, "We want sales today." He then would joyfully shout, "Since we are in agreement, God will answer our prayers." He had not read the entire passage. The sales manager was trying to hold God to a promise that God never made. Actually, trying to force God to perform through our actions is called witchcraft.

The entire passage says, "When sincere believers gather together, are at peace with each other and God, and are earnestly praying, God will be there with them." Now that is a very different meaning than what the sales manager was promoting.

The correct Scripture, our reliable source, has a lot of ifs. If they are sincere, baptized Christians, who are not in conflict with each other, who have no serious sins on their souls and are earnestly praying, then God will be there.

There are many lies. We cannot go into all of them. However, with some Scriptural study and movement toward our communicating God, you should be able to intuit many such lies.

I have been discussing a loving, merciful God who gives generously and favors His people. I have not made Him the warm fireside cozy friend that you can have a beer with when you feel like it. The prevailing lie is that Jesus is your friend. That makes Him equal to you. It humanizes Jesus to a position of genie to be used for your ends. By making Jesus broken and fragile, He has little to offer. Once again you have made yourself God.

If you indeed believe that God the Father, Jesus and the Holy Spirit are your friends, then it follows that it is okay to be angry toward any one or all of them. You get angry because you believe that they have failed you in some way. You had relied on God and He did not come through. That anger is a "preadolescent poor baby you" acting out. The assumption is that you feel that you know more than God, so you are justified in your anger. Being angry toward God is an enormous sin. You have dismissed God, made Him less than God, and made yourself God.

Jesus often spoke about friendship. At the Last Supper, Jesus called His apostles His friends. He was speaking only to the apostles. He was about to empower these men to continue His mission of reconciliation. He gave only these men and their successors, other bishops, the same authority that God had given to Him to speak on faith and morals. He was only speaking to that one group. You cannot take a limited conversation and apply into yourself. On other occasions, Jesus spoke about friendship but did not call any other group friends.

By lowering the Mystical to your level, the Mystical is of no value. God must be beyond your understanding or He is nothing.

CHAPTER 3
LIES THAT YOUR MAMA AND EVERYONE ELSE TOLD YOU
REFLECTIONS

A major theme of this book is establishing a trusting, intimate relationship with God. A difficulty in establishing such a relationship is your lack of trust in Him. Your lack of trust is a product of others' erroneous beliefs and your own misconceptions based on their and your inability to trust. I will include a reflection on trust. These reflections and others will help you to better understand yourself, thus preparing you to enter a deeper, more intimate relationship with your Creator.

Jesus could not forgive my sins. They are too many and too big. What troubles you? What are you afraid of? What do you worry about? How controlling are you?

Reflections on this chapter:

- Reread the chapter carefully.
- List what you believe are the main points.
  Which points trouble you the most?
- Why are they troubling?
- How have you addressed these troubling problems in the past?
- What can you do today to resolve these troubling problems?
- You may have had other thoughts not included in this chapter that you should address. What are they?
- How will you resolve them today?
- Write your own personal prayer to God regarding the above information.

- CHAPTER 4 -
WHO IS GOD AND HOW DOES HE OPERATE?

When you know God better, you will discover how He takes loving care of His creation. Scripture, your reliable source, will teach you how God works. I will focus on some of those points here.

You cannot understand God. Consequently, you speak in metaphors, thus assigning God human characteristics. Consequently, you have replaced the real God with your broken and frail god that is not trustworthy. Knowing about God is not the same as knowing God. Scripture gives you a hint of knowing about Him. You may come to know Him through intimate prayer and observation.

You go to the mystical and unexplainable when you are in need. It is actually better not to be able to fully explain God. Trying to understand mystery is the Western cultural approach. Its purpose is to control. If you were able to control God, He would have less appeal.

Scripture, your reliable source, and the teachings of the Church Fathers describe God as everlasting, all powerful, perfect, all knowing, forgiving, merciful and eager to give grace and pardon for your sins. God pursues you even in your own sinfulness and unwillingness to be interested in Him. God is described as always being the initiator of good. You are always the responder to good.

You, as a responder, are an important concept. If you think about God, if you pray, if you do a good work, if you empathize with or love your neighbor, if you get out of bed and struggle your way to Sunday church, it is all because He has inspired you to do so. Imagine the opportunity in being a responder. It can be a real occasion to know God. Imagine when you think of or do good, charitable and merciful things you are responding. If God can bring your narcissistic self to the point of caring for others, He must be worthy of your trust.

I remember sad moments when I was full of my pitiful self and wanted to sit around all day in my poor baby me. During one of my worst pitiful days, a man came to my door asking for food. He had lost his job and his family was in desperate need. I was nice to him, gave him food, but was still eager for him to leave so I could return to my pitiful self. On the way out of the door, he told me that a swarm of bees had stung his arm and he was in terrible pain. I really didn't want to hear it. I just wanted him to leave. No sooner than I had closed my door, God said, "Go pray for him. Don't let him leave until you have done so." Even my pitiful self could not say no to God. We prayed and his pain was instantly gone. Thank you, Lord. That true story clearly illustrates God being the initiator and me the responder.

God even pursues those who are running away from Him and are actually in terrible sin. While visiting a trailer park, one of the very poor residents complained about some new neighbors who were stealing from their neighbors. Surely God took the lead on this one. I courageously made my way to the thieves' trailer. I was met by three rugged individuals. We did the usual chit chat, and I learned that one of them was losing his sight. I asked if he would like to pray. He said yes. Before we prayed, I asked him what he could read from the newspaper. He could barely read the bold print. We prayed. The thief's eyes were healed. His sight returned. Now he was able to read the small newsprint. I embraced him and said, "See how much God loves you. Now stop stealing from your neighbors." It was later reported that all three reformed thieves became quite the helpers throughout the trailer park.

So please remember that if you even think a good thought or do a good deed, it is because God inspired you. All you did was to respond.

I have challenged a number of ministers on their approach to the salvation altar call. The words give the false impression that if we initiate something, then God will do something. It is not that way at all. The better approach would be for the minister to say, "God has always been relentlessly pursuing you. He is calling you to Himself. Respond to that call by coming forward and let us embrace you in His Precious Name."

You can see that God works through inspiration. He knows what is best for you. He graces you to freely choose His way.

The Ten Commandments are an excellent example of your communicating God speaking to you. Your lack of trust may lead you to believe that the commandments are limiting your choices and therefore your happiness. You have given into some lustful indulgences and have found that the outcomes were not as satisfying as you thought. As a matter of fact, they got you into a lot of trouble. So get over yourself and trust that the Ten Commandments are one of the many ways that God is looking after you. If you want to condense the Ten Commandments into two, then "love God with your whole heart and soul and your neighbor likewise." However, those two require more maturity than the ten.

Spiritual laws are derived from these commandments. They are inevitable whether you believe in them or not. You don't have to believe in gravity, but things do fall and that is that. Here are three fundamental spiritual laws that further illustrate how God works. God has told you in advance that these laws were meant for a blessing, but they could, if you choose, bring about suffering. That early warning endorses that God is not a trickster, and He can be trusted.

The first Spiritual Law is "What you sow, you shall reap." Some mistakenly call that karma. Let's call it "You asked for it, so you got it." Or call it consequences. You hate that word. You don't like consequences although consequences good or bad can teach little untrustworthy children about the trustworthy love of God. You have experienced reaping what you have sown. A very simple example might be putting food on the counter for the cats to eat. Consequently, the cats go to the counter to eat. Sometimes they eat your food that is also on the counter. You reap what was sown.

What you reap can be what others have sown. We are on the pilgrimage together. There is no such thing as a private sin. A good example is the financial greed of some manufacturers who put carcinogens into their products. You consume those products. You get cancer. You reap their sowing.

Get over yourself. You can stop blaming God for bad things and get on the backs of those greedy manufacturers and get them to change. Then you will reap the positive blessing of what you have sown.

You could develop other examples using drunken driving, molesters, adulterers, poor politicians and absent fathers.

You can sow good things and you would reap good things. These are not necessarily the same good thing but good nonetheless. You are also reaping the good things sown by every person throughout history, such as medicine, scientific advancement and even the writers of Scriptures.

You can attempt to play games with God by doing some good thing, expecting a super good thing in return.

You will receive the reward that God chooses. God is not a player.

An important aspect of sowing and reaping is that the longer it takes to get your reward or negative consequence, the greater it shall be. An example of delayed consequences might be child molestation. He or she molested a child and was never stopped by those who actually knew of the offence, and the child is afforded no justice or healing. The child, as an adult, still carried the pain and ultimately took that anger out by molesting other children and on and on it goes. It would have been better for the original molester to get his or her reaping early.

The second Spiritual Law is "Do not judge others." That quote is often misused. Examples: "You can't tell me what to do." "You don't know me." Or you use not rightly judging as an escape from responsibility. You are called to judge and speak on a wrong. However, you cannot judge the condition of someone's heart.

An example of judging someone's heart might be a father frequently pushing his overweight child off his lap because her excess weight is very painful. The child judges his heart by assuming that he does not love her. A consequence of judging someone's heart is that you may be judged for doing the same thing. In our illustration, the child who judged her father's heart as being unloving becomes herself hard hearted and, consequently, avoids close relationships, particularly with men.

The third Spiritual Law is "Honor your mother and your father and you will do well and prosper." You can see the sowing, reaping and do not judge the condition of another's heart built in to this commandment

For example, a father not being honorable has an affair and leaves his family. The entire family suffers and is insistent on holding on to their bitterness. Eventually, that family will fall apart and so will the children's families. You can honor such a situation by forgiving the father and growing in empathy. The father most likely did the abandonment from his own brokenness. Then they could ask God to bless their father. Difficult to do, I know, but necessary to pull out those tangled roots.

In summary, you can grow in your trust toward God when you realize just how much He loves you. He has shown His love by giving you His Son. Jesus showed His love through His life, death and resurrection. The Holy Spirit shows you His love by pursuing even the lost and initiating while still allowing your free will choices. God created the Spiritual Laws to show how you can benefit by choosing good over evil.

God indeed is looking out for you. He is trustworthy.

CHAPTER 4
WHO IS GOD AND HOW DOES HE OPERATE?
REFLECTIONS

A major theme of this book is establishing a trusting, intimate relationship with God. A difficulty in establishing such a relationship is your lack of trust in Him. Your lack of trust is a product of others' erroneous beliefs and your own misconceptions based on their and your inability to trust. I will include a reflection on trust. These reflections and others will help you to better understand yourself, thus preparing you to enter a deeper, more intimate relationship with your Creator.

When you feel powerless, how do you get your power back? What are your principal emotional resources, e.g., your checkbook, your employment, your social status?

Reflections on this chapter:

- Reread the chapter carefully.
- List what you believe are the main points.
  Which points trouble you the most?
- Why are they troubling?
- How have you addressed these troubling problems in the past?
- What can you do today to resolve these troubling problems?
- You may have had other thoughts not included in this chapter that you should address. What are they?
- How will you resolve them today?
- Write your own personal prayer to God regarding the above information.

- CHAPTER 5 -
SIN

I sincerely hope that my comments on sin will give you the opportunity not only to reflect on your personal history but also on the mercy and love of God. I will be discussing guilt, shame and sins surrounding divorce, marriage and sexuality. I have chosen these topics because they are of vital importance regarding trust.

The purpose here is to experience the forgiveness given to you by Jesus on the cross when He begged His Father to "forgive them for they know not what they are doing." You do not know, nor are you capable of knowing, the enormity of your sins including those little ones like stealing sweets from Grandma's candy drawer.

Not long ago, I saw the movie *Unplanned*. The protagonist, female lead character, had a lengthy history of managing an abortion clinic. Through the support of her husband and embrace of a local Christian advocacy group, she realized her sinfulness. She left her position and repented of her sins. One evening, she was painfully lamenting the enormity of killing over sixty thousand babies. She asked her husband how God could possibly forgive such an unworthy sinner as herself. His wonderfully simple but perfect answer was, "Because He is God."

You might have asked that or a similar question. The answer remains the same, "Because He is God." You cannot imagine or understand the love and mercy that God has for you.

You will never be worthy of anything regarding God. The fact is He has made you worthy through His crucified Son. So not only "get over it" but be joyful for His graciousness to make you worthy.

The only unforgivable sin is the one you fail to repent and confess.

All too frequently, I have had immature Christians sit before me asking if they are going to hell because of some terrible confessed sin that still haunts their conscience. They fear that they have abandoned God or that God has abandoned them. My heart breaks for their sorrow. I would warmly reply that our Good Lord has not abandoned them but rather has inspired them to come to Christian counselor who is also a priest. I remind them that they have responded to God's inspiration. They would not have responded if indeed they had abandoned God. Their fundamental option, what drives them the most, is still God. We would soon begin to pray together.

Similarly, you may be burdened by some sort of guilt. I remember an elderly lady visiting our counseling office just for a weekend. She was troubled and very anxious. We spoke for over an hour trying to sort things out. During our lunch break, I asked God how I could be of most help for this troubled woman. He said, "Ask her about her abortion."

After lunch, we met again. In a calm loving way, I simply said, "Tell me about your abortion." She broke down and cried for some time. Then she told the story that had been haunting her for thirty years. Yes, her guilt over killing her child was killing her. We spoke, she cried some more, prayed and finally asked God for forgiveness. At last, she was freed.

This woman was carrying objective guilt. By that, I mean she actually did something that was sinful, so she was guilty. That is the case for most of us. We actually did something wrong, so we are guilty.

Subjective guilt is something far different but also burdens many people. Subjective guilt happens when you judge yourself. You believe that you did something wrong.

You have written a rule book that is housed inside yourself entitled *How Life Should Go According to Me.* That book is highly subjective, and the rules written within are drawn from your interpretation of your early years and then supported by how you further judged life as you aged. You might have had a rather tragic experience or an experience that begins an addiction. Because of those terrible experiences, often you will stop emotionally maturing. You judge yourself guilty of something you thought you had done when in fact you have been a victim.

For example, let's say that you, as a young girl, believed that your emotionally absent father didn't love you. You might have written a rule that concludes that "not only your father but that all men are incapable of love." You might then have created another rule which could be "I must not allow myself to be vulnerable to men." Usually, rules come in groups that I nickname "cat hairballs." As you separate out the various, sometimes very tangled roots, you could find another rule that says, "I must be perfect if I stand even a chance to win a man's affections." So you find yourself afraid of men yet still wanting to be loved by a man. It is confusing.

In an effort to be perfect, either as a child or an adult, you might have done some questionable but not objectively sinful things to earn a man's love. You might have then judged yourself as not perfect. That is subjective guilt. Although it is not objective guilt, it can feel as painful.

You could have confessed subjective guilt and not have felt forgiven. If you have confessed the same guilt many times or have gone to the altar many times for the same reason, you could be suffering from subjective guilt. The Bible does not speak directly about subjective guilt. You will need counseling to sort out your rule book.

Shame can feel like objective or subjective guilt, but it is neither. Persons who feel shame believe that there is something fundamentally wrong with them. Consequently, they judge themselves as not good enough to be loved by anyone, human or divine. They believe that God would not forgive them.

Since shame is originally created by the individual's judgment upon their dysfunctional childhood, it is firmly rooted within themselves. You could love that person mightily, tell them to love and trust God and that God forgives them. They will not believe it because they do believe that they are just not good enough and something is fundamentally wrong with them. If shamed persons were surrounded by people whom they respected and they belonged to a loving faith community, in time, with patience and lots of prayer, they might grow out of their shame. It is comforting to know that God knows and has compassion for those who carry shame.

A Christian marriage has the opportunity to be a greenhouse for intimate relationships. All too often, it becomes a swamp filled with distrust and annihilation.

Most churches today regard marriage as permanent and divorce as a grievous fault, a sin. But certainly no church would force anyone to stay in an abusive marriage with an unrepentant abuser. Our reliable source, Scripture, directs us to live in peace. Neither Scripture nor a faith community would want the human Temple of the Holy Spirit abused in any way.

There are legitimate reasons for divorce beyond the traditional sin of adultery. If we were to understand adultery as unjustly breaking the marital vows, then justice would indicate that there would be other circumstances, just as serious, that could be legitimate reasons for divorce. The marriage covenant may be broken by sins defined in Holy Scripture as capital offenses, including murder, idolatry, adultery, homosexuality and witchcraft. We will all agree that a marriage is not only a sacred matter but the stability of marriage is the essence of the stability of our culture. Marriage is very serious, and taking it otherwise is a sin in itself.

Not all marriages are truly Christian marriages. Points to consider:

1. While every marriage properly performed by an authorized person is indeed a legal contract, mostly to do business together, it may not be a sacramental, Christian marriage. We believe that in a Christian marriage, one if not both members are earnestly practicing Christians.

2. The officiating Christian minister shall have ascertained the right of the parties to contract marriage according to the laws of the state in which the marriage is to take place. No officiating person, minister or otherwise, can validly marry anyone who is outside of civil law.

3. The officiating Christian minister shall have ascertained that both parties understand that Holy Matrimony is a spiritual and physical union between a man and a woman who freely enter by mutual consent of heart, mind, and will and with the full intent to enter the union will be a lifelong commitment.

The expressed intent of entering a lifelong union is required. If even one member of the union has the intent, spoken or unspoken, "to let's just try this out and see if it works" or even thinks this is a game, or they are drunk or high on something, this is not a Christian marriage.

"By mutual consent" means that neither person feels forced by anyone, circumstances, or emotional difficulties, fraud or are mistaken as to the identity or character of the partner.

This would rule out "shotgun" weddings or being coerced because of pregnancy or other coercions.

The "knowledge of whom you are marrying" goes beyond an imposter; it goes to the character of the person whom you are marrying.

While you do not know the future and you accept the other "for better or for worse," there are reasonable expectations. For example, if one person of the couple expressed a real desire to have children and the other secretly withheld that they are not able to have children, that would be fraud. Additionally, if they did not reveal that they had an active sexual addiction such as pornography or another addiction, or were transsexual, or homosexual, or had or were suffering from a mental illness such as bipolar disorder that would be fraudulent.

On one occasion a man craftily manipulated a woman into believing that he truly loved her. He was very kind and generous. She was overwhelmed into feeling secure and wanted. Soon after the marriage, it became obvious that his intention was to use her money and credit to rebuild his floundering business. Once his business was stabilized, he left her without notice and deep in financial debt.

Another less obvious example was a "good Christian man" who had manipulated his wife-to-be into believing that he loved God and that they had the loving endorsement of his church community. The woman was too quickly enamored and didn't recognize that she was his narcissistic victory. He captured a needy woman that he could manipulate thus avoiding responsibility for his own pathologies. It took eight terrible and abusive years of marriage and four torturous years of counseling for her to realize the truth of her situation. Finally, she left the marriage. Such a union would not be a Christian marriage.

All too often, I hear brides say, "I didn't really know who this man was." "I was scared, was I making the right decision?" "All my friends were there and we spent all this money, I just have to go through with it." This would not be a valid Christian marriage.

Hopefully the officiating Christian minister had looked into all these things at least six months prior to the wedding date.

I believe also that a Christian marriage must be officiated, witnessed and solemnized by a valid Christian minister who does so in accordance with civil law and the canons of his church. A Justice of the Peace or an online "ordained minister" or any such person, while they might be able to officiate legally, does not have the credentials to officiate a Christian marriage.

The above information may be entirely new to you. In any case, do not take the above as a rationalization to give yourself an automatic excuse to terminate your marriage. If indeed your marriage is troubled, then receive some Christian counseling from a professional Christian counselor. Warning, most ministers are not qualified nor have the time to devote to long term counseling.

I do believe that if a troubled couple spent as much time, money and energy into their existing marriage as they would have in a divorce, reestablishing their lives, and living four plus years in the aftermath of emotional, financial, social pain, and a lifetime of pain for the children, they could have transformed their troubled marriage into a victorious celebration. If everyone took marriage much more seriously and do the positive things that I have mentioned above, there would be far fewer divorces.

Sex is one of those two-edged swords. It can draw you closer to God or to hell's gate. If Jesus were watching, would you masturbate? Would you get naked and use your opposite sex partner for your own pleasure? Would you put yourself in a situation that might create lifelong negative consequences? Would you put yourself and possibly others at risk of a venereal disease? Would you abort a baby? Would you look at pornography? Would you make naked videos or photos? Would you be so selfish to first seek out your pleasure, comfort or anything else knowing that you are putting another nail into Christ on the Cross?

If you were to say, "Sure, why not?" get on your knees now because you are in serious trouble. Remember God is not attempting to take away your free will or hamper you in any way. The fact is that He already knows what will hurt you and damage your relationship with your Creator. Now that is a trustworthy statement found not only in your common sense but also in your reliable source, Scripture.

Masturbation is the tangled root of many evils. I, all too often, hear from parents that their teenagers' masturbation is just a normal way of discovering their sexuality. Now that's pop psychology! The truth is your sexuality is a marital function that leads toward emotional and spiritual intimacy with openness to fostering children with a person of the opposite gender. True intimacy can only be found with Christ in the middle of a permanent trusting relationship in which both parties feel safe to grow and allow such intimacy.

Masturbation then is purposeful self-stimulation for self-centered pleasure. The act is often accompanied with sexual fantasy and can promote social isolation.

Masturbation is the doorway to other sinful acts such as pornography, rape, devaluing the opposite sex, prostitution, and various addictions not limited to sexual addiction but also including homosexuality and it even sets the stage for murdering babies.

Modern science has validated all the above statements. God knew all this from the very beginning. Sexual intercourse outside of marriage is a form of mutual masturbation. It attacks the dignity of the persons involved and the sanctity of marriage. Repeat after me: "I believe that I love my mate so much that it gives me license to affront her or his dignity, thus turning what was intended to be sacred within a marriage into sacrilege and threatening our dating relationship and certainly, if we were to marry, jeopardizing our marriage." If you can honestly say that, get on your knees because you are in big trouble and you are threatening those around you.

Living together, also called playing house, has been supported by a number of rationalizations. "Let's have a trial, living together." "We will learn who the other person really is up close." "It will help in caring for our baby and help with our finances." "If it doesn't work, no harm, no foul."

If our rationalizations are logical, wise and founded on sacrificial altruism, why does God call it a sin? Simply living together, regardless of the reason, will ultimately have numerous difficulties. It diminishes your personal and relational dignity. It is a poor rationalization for using each other. Playing house is not marriage. Living together does not mirror marriage. Your marital vows will immediately make your entire earthly, spiritual and emotional realities different. Previous to marriage, your negotiations to get along were essentially selfish maneuvers to get what you wanted. It does not resemble a selfless sacrificial love that you willingly give to your life partner. Marriages birthed from these utility relationships are often fraught with insecurities, jealousies and a decided lack of trust. After all, if you play at marriage, you are liable to be unfaithful when married.

My experience validates that sinful premarital relationships have a higher divorce rate than typically well-founded Christian marriages. It would be foolish to take lightly what God holds as sacred. I understand that what I just said can be difficult to hear. But sugar preaching does no good. If you are in questionable situations, I would encourage you to speak with a Christian counselor or your pastor whom you have placed as guardian of your soul.

You cannot live a life that essentially rejects God and have an intimate relationship with Him at the same time.

CHAPTER 5
SIN
REFLECTIONS

A major theme of this book is establishing a trusting, intimate relationship with God. A difficulty in establishing such a relationship is your lack of trust in Him. Your lack of trust is a product of others' erroneous beliefs and your own misconceptions based on their and your inability to trust. I will include a reflection on trust. These reflections and others will help you to better understand yourself, thus preparing you to enter a deeper, more intimate relationship with your Creator.

Has God ever asked you to do something absolutely incredible? If you were asked, what was your response? Could God trust you to do something really *important?*

Reflections on this chapter:

- Reread the chapter carefully.
- List what you believe are the main points.
  Which points trouble you the most?
- Why are they troubling?
- How have you addressed these troubling problems in the past?
- What can you do today to resolve these troubling problems?
- You may have had other thoughts not included in this chapter that you should address. What are they?
- How will you resolve them today?
- Write your own personal prayer to God regarding the above information.

-CHAPTER 6-
FOUR MODELS OF EXAMINATION OF CONSCIENCE

As you reflect upon this self-examination, ask the Lord to grant you the virtues, contrary to your vices (sins). For example, if you struggle with purity, ask for courage, strength, patience, discipline, and charity!

The First Commandment: I am the LORD your God, You shall have no other gods before me.

Have I sinned against God by seriously believing in New Age, Scientology, astrology, horoscopes, fortune-telling, superstition or engaging in the occult? Did I endanger my faith or cause scandal by associating with anti-Christian groups and associations (e.g., the Freemasons)? Have fame, fortune, money, career, pleasure, etc. replaced God as my highest priority? Have I neglected my daily prayers? Have I performed my duties toward God reluctantly or grudgingly? Did I seriously doubt in matters of faith? Do I worship the false gods of status, consumerism, or peer approval? Do I ignore or avoid old friends in order to be part of the popular crowd? Do I give support to my peers when they tell racial or ethnic jokes? Do I feel indifferent toward the poor and thinking them losers by social standards? Do I find it hard to see the value in those who are different from me?

The Second Commandment: You shall not take the name of the Lord in vain.

Have I committed blasphemy by using the name of God and Jesus Christ to swear rather than to praise? Have I committed sacrilege by showing disrespect to holy objects (cross or crucifix) or contempt for religious persons (bishop, priests, deacons, monks, pastors, women religious) or for sacred places (in Church)? Have I neglected to support the Church and the poor by sharing my time, talent, and treasure? Did I do my best to fulfill the vows, promises and resolutions that I made to God? Did I break private or public vows? Do I use profane language? Is this choice prompted by the violence of the vocabulary, its low opinion of others or its insulting character?

The Third Commandment: Remember the Sabbath day to keep it holy.

Have I missed going to church on any Sunday without good reason such as dangerous weather, being sick, taking care of the sick or having to travel a great distance? Have I shown disrespect by leaving church early or arriving late, not paying attention, or not joining in the prayers? Did I do unnecessary work on Sunday, which could have been done the day before? Have I been stingy in my support for the Church? Do I give of my time and talent?

The Fourth Commandment: Honor your father and your mother, that your days may be long in the land which the Lord your God gives you.

Parents: Have I set a bad example for my children by casually missing church, neglecting prayer or ignoring my responsibility to provide a Christian education? Do I show little or no interest in my children's faith and practice of it? Have I shown disrespect for those in authority, government or church? Have I not expressed my moral values to them?

Children: Have I been disobedient or disrespectful to my parents or guardians? Did I neglect to help them with household chores? Have I caused them unnecessary worry and anxiety by my attitude, behavior, moods, etc.? Did I feel hurt and react proudly when I was corrected by them? Did I quarrel with my brothers and sisters? Do I thank my parents for what they do for me? Do I offer to help around the house, or do I see myself as a guest?

(If your parents are divorced, separated or widowed) Do I try to understand their pain or loneliness? Why do I try to impress others and yet have little sense of the needs of those in my family?

The Fifth Commandment: You shall not kill.

Did I consent, recommend, advise, approve, support or have an abortion? Did I actively or passively cooperate with an act of euthanasia whereby ordinary means were stopped or means taken to directly end the life of an elderly or sick person? Have I committed an act of violence or abuse (physical, sexual, emotional or verbal)? Have I endangered the lives of others by reckless driving or by driving under the influence of drugs or alcohol? Do I show contempt for my body by neglecting to take care of my own health? Have I been mean or unjust to anyone? Have I held a grudge or sought revenge against someone who wronged me? Do I point out others' faults and mistakes while ignoring my own? Do I complain more than I compliment? Am I ungrateful for what other people do for me? Do I tear people down rather than encourage them? Am I prejudiced against people because of their color, language, or ethnic-religious background? Why do I feel the need to control or humiliate someone I claim to care about? Did I easily get angry or lose my temper? Am I envious or jealous of others? How many persons have I led to sin? Did I get drunk or take prohibited drugs or misuse drugs? When someone offends me, do I desire revenge, harbor enmity, hatred or ill feelings? Did I ask pardon whenever I offended anyone? Did I insult or tease others?

The Sixth Commandment: You shall not commit adultery.

Do I use other persons for my own selfish pleasure? Do I lie to get sex or force others to act against their values? Do I see sex as a way to be popular or to rebel against my parents? Did I entertain indecent thoughts? Did I consent to evil desires against the virtue of purity, even though I may not have carried them out? Did I engage in or start impure conversations? Do I take care of those details of modesty and decency, which are the safeguards of purity? Did I lead others to sins of impurity or immodesty? Did I masturbate? Do I have friendships which are habitual occasions of sin? Do I degrade human love by confusing it with selfishness or pleasure? Did I engage in sexual acts with others that were sinful?

(For married people) Did I make improper use of marriage? Did I deprive my spouse of his or her marital right? Did I betray conjugal fidelity in desire or in deed? Did I use birth control after new life had been conceived (IUD, morning after pills, abortion)?

The Seventh Commandment: You shall not steal.

Do I cheat? Do I shoplift or take things belonging to others? Did I steal any object or money? Did I cause damage to another's property? Did I harm anyone by deception, fraud or coercion in business contracts or transactions? Did I spend beyond my means? Do I give alms according to my capacity? Did I neglect to pay my debts? Did I retain things found or stolen? Did I desire to steal? Am I diligent in my work and studies or do I give in to laziness or love of comfort? Was I greedy? Do I have an excessively materialistic view of life?

The Eighth Commandment: You shall not bear false witness.

Have I told a lie in order to deceive someone? Have I told the truth with the purpose and intention of ruining someone's reputation (sin of detraction)? Have I told a lie or spread rumors, which may ruin someone's reputation (sin of calumny or slander)? Did I commit perjury by falsely swearing an oath on the Bible? Am I a busybody or do I love to spread gossip and secrets about others? Do I love to hear bad news about my enemies? Can I be trusted to keep a confidence after I promise? Do I lie to protect my own ego even if someone will be hurt?

The Ninth Commandment: You shall not desire for another's spouse.

Did I have any sex before or outside of marriage? Do I view pornographic material (magazines, videos, Internet, hotlines)? Have I gone to massage parlors or adult bookstores? Did I commit the sin of masturbation? Have I not avoided the occasions of sin (persons or places) which would tempt me to be unfaithful to my spouse or to my own chastity? Do I encourage and entertain impure thoughts and desires? Do I tell or listen to dirty jokes? Have I committed fornication or adultery?

The Tenth Commandment: You shall not desire for another's goods.

Have I stolen any object, committed any shoplifting, or cheated anyone of their money? Did I knowingly deceive someone in business or commit fraud? Have I shown disrespect or even contempt for other people's property? Have I done any acts of vandalism? Am I greedy or envious of another's goods? Do I let financial and material concerns or the desire for comfort override my duty to God, to the Church, to my family or to my own spiritual well-being? Am I envious of others? Do I resent their popularity or success? Do I feel that I have to put others down in order to feel better about myself? Do I resent my parents when they tell me that they cannot afford to buy the things that I feel I need to keep up with my friends?

IMITATE THE FAITH OF THE MAGI AND FOLLOW THEIR PATH EXAMINATION OF CONSCIENCE FOR LAY PERSONS

Guided by the star, the Magi reach Bethlehem. They enter the house, which they recognize by the pointing star that stands over the place where the child was. They find the child with his mother, but a mother who is a virgin.

Where do you find Jesus? Do you find Jesus in the most unusual places such as your wife, children, friends and family? When people look at you, do they see Jesus? When your wife or loved ones look at you, do they look up or away? Do they seek you out for comfort and guidance, or do they imagine that you are not really interested? Do your children and wife treat you respectfully? Do you always treat your family respectfully?

The Magi fell down and worshiped him. Do you do likewise? The Magi, experts in divine worship, teach you how you are to worship God. Luke says: They fell down and worshiped him. But that is not how you act: rather, when you enter the house of prayer, the house in which we pray to Jesus, do you immediately collapse or sit down, overpowered by your idleness or negligence as by a heavy load; then, carelessly, or even eagerly, you settle yourself not for prayer but for sleep? Not only do you not kneel for prayer, but you yawn and scratch yourself, and you cast your wandering gaze now up, now down. As for the prayers themselves if they are to be called prayers and the psalms, you run through them so quickly that you cut the verses short by half.

Have you ever prostrated before the Lord? Can you see Jesus as both your friend and your God? Do you pray to your friend? How often do you pray? Do you look forward to raising your heart and mind to God? Is prayer just one more thing that you have to find time for in your hurried world? Is your prayer rushed? Sometimes do you just listen? When you go to church, is it to worship? Do you spend time socializing when you should be praying? Is Sunday worship your weekly fill up? Who is the center of the Lord's Day? Do you dress as "come as you are" or the best you can to honor God? When you return home, do you discuss the sermon with your wife, children or family? Does the sermon go beyond the exit of the church? How do you live out your Christian faith? What is your definition of a Christian?

Imitate the Magi, who fell down and worshiped him. The text goes on to say: Opening their treasures, they offered him gifts. Think of the wonderful faith of the Magi: they saw before them an infant wrapped in rags and lying in an unworthy inn that was probably a wretched shack; they saw a mother clothed in the cheap garments of the people, her reputation further blackened because of the work done by her carpenter husband; they saw, finally, the carpenter himself, unkempt from his manual toil and labor as a carpenter, and yet called the father of so mighty a king. The Magi saw all this, and yet they did not lose heart nor think that they had journeyed foolishly and in vain; they did not even think to themselves: "Is this poor infant, this child of the people, to become the King of the Jews? Was it for such a child that we have travelled this long road? How shall so poor, humble, and lowly a child rise to royal honors? We regret our toil; we are disgusted with our journey. Let us at least take back with us the gifts we brought.

The Magi entertained none of these thoughts. Instead, made certain by the grace given them of the royal and divine majesty of the child, they fell humbly down and adored, and then opened their treasures and joyfully offered gold, frankincense, and myrrh.

How many times have you been disappointed in God? Do you accuse Him of not being there for you? Are bad things His fault? After all, if He was really there, bad things would not have happened. When you look for God, where do you find Him? Have you worked really hard at something and got upset because it didn't work out the way you wanted it to? When God asks you to do something difficult, what do you do? Do you not do it at all or simply put it off until it is forgotten? When you see a poor dusty beggar, what are your first thoughts? When your teenaged child acts out, what do you see? What do you say to the child? Does changing diapers have anything to do with God? What are your concerns about tithing? If God were to tell you to leave everything behind and go follow Him, what would be your response?

From a sermon by Julian of Vezelay
(Sermon 11: SC 192, 80–85)

Imitate the Faith of the Magi and Follow Their Path Examination of Conscience for Clergy

Guided by the star, the Magi reach Bethlehem. They enter the house, which they recognize by the pointing star that stands over the place where the child was. They find the child with his mother, but a mother who is a virgin.

What was your journey to follow your vocation? What was the most difficult part of that journey? Do you sometimes wish that you were not ordained? If so, what would your life look like? Where do you find Jesus? Do you find Jesus in the most unusual places? When people look at you in your clerics, do they see Jesus? When others appreciate that you are Christ present for them, do they seek you out for comfort and guidance, or do they imagine that you are not really interested? Do you treat your Presiding Bishop as Christ present for you? Are you engaged with other clerics in your jurisdiction?

The Magi fell down and worshiped him. Do you do likewise? The Magi, experts in divine worship, teach you how you are to worship God. Luke says: "They fell down and worshiped him." But that is not how you act: rather, when you enter the house of prayer, the house in which we pray to Jesus, you immediately collapse or sit down, overpowered by your idleness or negligence as by a heavy load; then, carelessly, or even eagerly, you settle yourself not for prayer but for sleep. Not only do you not kneel for prayer, but you yawn and scratch yourself, and you cast your wandering gaze now up, now down. As for the prayers themselves if they are to be called prayers and the psalms, you run through them so quickly that you cut the verses short by half.

Have you ever prostrated before the Lord? How often do you kneel? How often do you pray? Do you look forward to raising your heart and mind to God? Is prayer just one more thing that you have to find time for in your hurried world? Is your prayer rushed? Sometimes do you just sit quietly and listen? How often do you use a prayer book? Do you read sacred writers? When you officiate at a service, is it also a worship experience for you? How often do you fast? How do you live out your faith tradition? What is your definition of a bishop, priest, deacon, minister? Would other people define you according to that definition? Do you treat all things as if they were items on the altar? Is your sanctuary and all items within it clean? Do you allow lay persons to handle sacred items? Before a service, do you take a moment of prayer? How do the people you serve address you? Does that address remind them of your special divine role in their lives? How much time do you spend as a social worker or secretary? Do you feel as though you are the guardian of your community's souls?

Imitate the Magi, who fell down and worshiped him. The text goes on to say: Opening their treasures, they offered him gifts. Think of the wonderful faith of the Magi: they saw before them an infant wrapped in rags and lying in an unworthy inn that was probably a wretched shack; they saw a mother clothed in the cheap garments of the people, her reputation further blackened because of the work done by her carpenter husband; they saw, finally, the carpenter himself, unkempt from his manual toil and labor as a carpenter, and yet called the father of so mighty a king. The Magi saw all this, and yet they did not lose heart nor think that they had journeyed foolishly and in vain; they did not even think to themselves: "Is this poor infant, this child of the people, to become the King of the Jews? Was it for such a child that we have travelled this long road? How shall so poor, humble, and lowly a child rise to royal honors? We regret our toil; we are disgusted with our journey. Let us at least take back with us the gifts we brought.

The Magi entertained none of these thoughts. Instead, made certain by the grace given them of the royal and divine majesty of the child, they fell humbly down and adored, and then opened their treasures and joyfully offered gold, frankincense, and myrrh.

Do some shameful things from your past hold you back? If you are criticized, justly or not, how do you respond? How many times have you been disappointed in God? Do you accuse Him of not being there for you? Do you believe that if you were good enough, God would be induced to answer your prayers? When you look for God, where do you find Him? Have you worked really hard at something and gotten upset because things did not work out the way you wanted? When God requires you to do something difficult, what do you do? Do you appreciate that your Presiding Bishop has the authority to ask you to do something rather difficult? If he did ask you to do a difficult thing, what would you do? When you see a poor dusty beggar, what are your first thoughts? What are your concerns about personal tithing?

From a sermon by Julian of Vezelay
(Sermon 11: SC 192, 80–85)

IMITATE THE FAITH OF THE MAGI AND FOLLOW THEIR PATH EXAMINATION OF CONSCIENCE FOR RELIGIOUS

Guided by the star, the Magi reach Bethlehem. They enter the house, which they recognize by the pointing star that stands over the place where the child was. They find the child with his mother, but a mother who is a virgin.

Where do you find Jesus? Do you find Jesus in the most unusual places? When people look at you in your habit, do they see Jesus? Do others seem to be drawn to you for no apparent reason? Do they seek you out for comfort and guidance, or do they imagine that you are not really interested? Do you treat your Abbot as Christ present for you? Are you engaged with other religious and your community?

The Magi fell down and worshiped him. Do you do likewise? The Magi, experts in divine worship, teach you how you are to worship God. Luke says: "They fell down and worshiped him." But that is not how you act: rather, when you enter the house of prayer, the house in which we pray to Jesus, you immediately collapse or sit down, overpowered by your idleness or negligence as by a heavy load; then, carelessly, or even eagerly, you settle yourself not for prayer but for sleep. Not only do you not kneel for prayer, but you yawn and scratch yourself, and you cast

your wandering gaze now up, now down.
As for the prayers themselves if they are to
be called prayers and the psalms, you run
through them so quickly that you cut the
verses short by half.

Have you ever prostrated before the Lord? How often
do you kneel? How often do you pray? Do you look
forward to raising your heart and mind to God? Is prayer
just one more thing that you have to find time for in your
hurried world? Is your prayer rushed? Sometimes do you
just listen? How often do you use a prayer book? Do you
read sacred writers? When you go to church, is it to
worship? Do you spend time socializing when you should
be praying? Is Sunday worship your weekly fill up? Who
is the center of the Lord's Day? How often do you fast?
Does your Lectio Divina include conversation? How do
you live out the Cistercian charism? What is your
definition of a Cistercian monk? Would other people
define you according to that definition? Do you treat all
things as if they were items on the altar?

Imitate the Magi, who fell down and
worshiped him. The text goes on to say:
Opening their treasures, they offered him
gifts. Think of the wonderful faith of the
Magi: they saw before them an infant
wrapped in rags and lying in an unworthy
inn that was probably a wretched shack;
they saw a mother clothed in the cheap
garments of the people, her reputation
further blackened because of the work
done by her carpenter husband; they saw,
finally, the carpenter himself, unkempt
from his manual toil and labor as a

carpenter, and yet called the father of so mighty a king. The Magi saw all this, and yet they did not lose heart nor think that they had journeyed foolishly and in vain; they did not even think to themselves: "Is this poor infant, this child of the people, to become the King of the Jews? Was it for such a child that we have travelled this long road? How shall so poor, humble, and lowly a child rise to royal honors? We regret our toil; we are disgusted with our journey. Let us at least take back with us the gifts we brought.

The Magi entertained none of these thoughts. Instead, made certain by the grace given them of the royal and divine majesty of the child, they fell humbly down and adored, and then opened their treasures and joyfully offered gold, frankincense, and myrrh.

How many times have you been disappointed in God? Do you accuse Him of not being there for you? Do you believe that if you were good enough, God would be induced to answer your prayers? When you look for God, where do you find Him? Have you worked really hard at something and gotten upset because it didn't work out the way you wanted it to? When God asks you to do something difficult, what do you do? If your Abbot were to ask you to do a difficult thing, what would you do? Do you ignore it or simply put it off until it is forgotten? When you see a poor dusty beggar, what are your first thoughts? What are your concerns about tithing? If God were to tell you to leave everything behind and go follow Him, what would be your response?

From a sermon by Julian of Vezelay
(Sermon 11: SC 192, 80–85)

CHAPTER 6
FOUR MODELS OF EXAMINATION OF CONSCIENCE
REFLECTIONS

A major theme of this book is establishing a trusting, intimate relationship with God. A difficulty in establishing such a relationship is your lack of trust. Your lack of trust is a product of others' erroneous beliefs and your own misconceptions based on their and your inability to trust. I will include a reflection on trust. These reflections and others will help you to better understand yourself, thus preparing you to enter a deeper, more intimate relationship with your Creator.

If God the Father told you that He highly favored you and that you were to do something that would change everything for all time, how would you respond?

Reflections on this chapter:

- Reread the chapter carefully.
- List what you believe are the main points.
  Which points trouble you the most?
- Why are they troubling?
- How have you addressed these troubling problems in the past?
- What can you do today to resolve these troubling problems?
- You may have had other thoughts not included in this chapter that you should address. What are they?
- How will you resolve them today?
- Write your own personal prayer to God regarding the above information.

- CHAPTER 7 -
PERSONAL TRANSFORMATION

One of my great joys is hearing my clients proclaim that they have become different people. They no longer think about or are influenced by what used to control them. They see the world entirely differently. I enjoy hearing couples describe how their marriages that were once painful are now a source of new life. How did they move from serious problems to such a transformation?

Let's start from the beginning. A broken and fragile person or marriage comes into counseling, terrorized, helpless and hopeless because of their multitude of sins. Their first assignment is to pray frequently together the twenty-third psalm. Their life is the valley of the shadow of death. I remind them that God's rod and staff will comfort and protect them. The psalm concludes with their Merciful Creator serving them a picnic. On the other side of the river is their defeated enemy. God and I are assuring them that they do not stand alone. Together, we go down a sometimes long and difficult road to becoming the new man, the new marriage.

They confess and are released from their many destructive sins. Asking for and receiving forgiveness is not enough. Just stopping the behavior is not enough. A transformation is needed.

Amendment necessitates walking, living and pursuing the forgiveness that they have already received. Transformation into the new man begins with controlling thoughts and temptations. Temptations whether of the flesh or Satan are where sins begin. Remember our reliable source; Scripture says that with God's help, all temptations can be conquered.

Often temptations are inspired by our erroneous beliefs. With sexual addictions, as well as other problems such as depression, anxiety or even anger the person believes that they are bad and unworthy persons. If anyone really knew them, they would most certainly be rejected. Therefore, they can't go to anyone to meet their needs.

In the case of a sexual addict they believe that sex is their most important need. Intimate and transparent relationships are very frightening, so they hide out in their addiction. In the early stages of sexual addiction, pornography is their hiding place. Pornography gives a semblance of a relationship that they can control and requires nothing from them.

The person who only stops the sinful behaviors, whatever they might be, is still influenced by these erroneous beliefs and consequently is still inclined to repeat to repeat them.

These debilitating beliefs originated in the person's dysfunctional family of origin. For example many boys are first introduced to pornography when they discover their father's or their friend's porn. Some young persons are sexual molested which can lead to a number of extremely destructive behaviors.

The case of a sex addict and co-addict, often the wife, the often have the very same beliefs; only they play them out differently. The wife believes poorly about herself and is fearful of a truly intimate and transparent relationship, so she does not really speak her needs. Because of this caution, she only wants the intimacy of marital sex when certain conditions are met and she feels safe. So she appears not to want sex. Meanwhile, the sexual addict husband wants it all the time. They suffer from the same beliefs but show them through opposite behaviors. It is wonderful to see the couple's eyes open when they finally understand their shared disabilities.

You can see the difficult pilgrimage to transform such deeply rooted thoughts not only in yourself but often with those around you. Such temptations influence your ability to be intimate with your Creator. True intimacy and ability to listen to God may mean transforming your entire household. The creation of a domestic church would be an excellent beginning.

Once again our reliable source, Scripture, gives instruction on transformation of thoughts and behaviors. St. Paul, in his letters, gives this example: He asks, "When is a liar no longer a liar?" He answers, "When the liar becomes a truth teller." You stop one behavior by doing the opposite behavior. When you do the opposite behavior, you are challenged by the emotional, spiritual and psychological efforts that become necessary to make the change. You often lie because you believe that is how you might be accepted by others. Liars generally think poorly about themselves. It is scary to be truthful. But when you discover that you are accepted more by being honest, then fear goes away.

Sometimes you have to be creative to determine the opposite behavior. For example, St. Paul asks, "When is a thief no longer a thief?" He says, "A thief is no longer a thief when he works for a living and gives to the poor." Usually, a thief steals for fear of lack. Working for a living eases the fear of lack. Giving to the poor can encourage gratitude for what you actually do have. Fear of tithing is essentially the same experience.

Believing that you are a bad and unworthy person comes from accepting your own or another's judgment upon yourself. The opposite behavior would be judging yourself as God judges you. Believing that you dare not be honest and transparent because you don't trust people is transformed when you first trust God. You cannot trust people until you trust God. That is one more reason why developing an intimate, listening relationship with God is so very important.

I have illustrated the transformation process using sexual addiction. The same process of confession and use of opposite behaviors works well for most problems.

For example, you could replace the seven deadly sins with holy virtues.

- *Pride—Humility*
- *Envy—Kindness*
- *Wrath—Patience*
- *Sloth—Diligence*
- *Avarice—Temperance*
- *Lust—Chastity*
- *Gluttony—Abstinence*

CHAPTER 7
PERSONAL TRANSFORMATION
REFLECTIONS

A major theme of this book is establishing a trusting, intimate relationship with God. A difficulty in establishing such a relationship is your lack of trust in Him. Your lack of trust is a product of others' erroneous beliefs and your own misconceptions based on their and your inability to trust. I will include a reflection on trust. These reflections and others will help you to better understand yourself, thus preparing you to enter a deeper, more intimate relationship with your Creator.

When someone changes your life without your consent, what do you do? Can that be an act of trust in them, believing that it is for your best interests, or does it seem like an intrusion into your freedoms?

Reflections on this chapter:

- Reread the chapter carefully.
- List what you believe are the main points. Which points trouble you the most?
- Why are they troubling?
- How have you addressed these troubling problems in the past?
- What can you do today to resolve these troubling problems?
- You may have had other thoughts not included in this chapter that you should address. What are they?
- How will you resolve them today?
- Write your own personal prayer to God regarding the above information.

- CHAPTER 8 -
CHRIST THE KING

This morning, I prayed from *The Liturgy of the Hours*. I was inspired to take excerpts from this day's reading. They perfectly respond to your pilgrimage of growing in trust toward God. Today is the Feast of Christ the King. Most of the readings describe how Christ uses His kingly authority. When you think about a king, it is easy to think of oppressive authority. And if you are an American, you just hate being told what to do. You will see through these excerpts that Christ as King is a much different experience. The God here is not of our making, drawn from our brokenness and fragility. Rather, Christ the King is strong, assured and extremely loving. He is worthy of your trust.

Now for some excerpts.

From antiphons

> We will call him peace maker, and his throne shall stand for ever.
> All the tribes of the earth will be blessed in him; all the nations will glorify him.
> They will sing his praises to the ends of the earth, and he will be their peace.

Excerpts from the various psalms

From the dust he lifts up the lowly.
From misery he raises the poor to set them in the company of princes. To the childless wife he gives a home and gladdens her heart with children. (Psalm 113)

Strong is his love for us;
He is faithful forever. (Psalm 117)

Blessed are they who put trust in God.
(Psalm 2)

May he defend the poor of the people and
save the children of the needy and crush the
oppressor. (Psalm 72)

O God, you are my God, for you I long; for
you my soul is thirsting. I gaze on you in the
sanctuary to see your strength and your
glory. For your love is better than life, my lips
will speak your praise. (Psalm 63)

For the Lord takes delight in his people.
He crowns the poor with salvation.
Let the faithful rejoice in their glory, shout for
joy and take their rest. (Psalm 149)

**These excerpts are taken from various hymns,
songs, and spiritual fathers.**

Hymn

Has blessed us on our way
With countless gifts of love,
Preserve us in his grace
And guide us in distress
And free us from all sin
Till heaven we possess.

Psalm-prayers

Lord, from the rising of the sun to its setting your name is worthy of praise.

Lord, we humbly ask for your goodness.

May you help us to hope in you,

Lord, you are the fullness of life, of holiness and of joy. Fill our days and nights with love of your wisdom, that we may bear fruit in the beauty of holiness, like a tree watered by running streams.

Father, creator of unfailing light, give the same light to those who call to you.

We put our trust in your faithfulness and proclaim the wonderful truths of salvation

May your loving kindness embrace us now and forever.

On Prayer by Origen, priest

For God is in each of his holy ones. Anyone who is holy obeys the spiritual laws of God who dwells in him as in a well-ordered city.

Thus the kingdom of God within us, as we continue to make progress will reach its highest point when the Apostle's words are fulfilled.

The kingdom of God cannot exist alongside the reign of sin.

Christ the King is the God that I want. He is gentle while authoritative, firm, strong, wise, and trustworthy. He loves me and raises me up to take part in His kingship.

There is a lot of getting over yourself, tangled roots to pull, and painful tilling the soil. Confession of sins is necessary. Your pilgrimage will be well worth it.

Scripture quotes taken from *The New American Bible.*

CHAPTER 8
CHRIST THE KING
REFLECTIONS

A major theme of this book is establishing a trusting, intimate relationship with God. A difficulty in establishing such a relationship is your lack of trust in Him. Your lack of trust is a product of others' erroneous beliefs and your own misconceptions based on their and your inability to trust. I will include a reflection on trust. These reflections and others will help you to better understand yourself, thus preparing you to enter a deeper, more intimate relationship with your Creator.

What kind of changes do you have to make to not only accept and forgive but to move into a new and better relationship with someone who has offended you?

Reflections on this chapter:

- Reread the chapter carefully.
- List what you believe are the main points. Which points trouble you the most?
- Why are they troubling?
- How have you addressed these troubling problems in the past?
- What can you do today to resolve these troubling problems?
- You may have had other thoughts not included in this chapter that you should address. What are they?
- How will you resolve them today?
- Write your own personal prayer to God regarding the above information.

- CHAPTER 9 -
PRAYER CONCERNS

So far, we have taken a look at getting over ourselves and pulling up tangled roots. Now we will study building a foundation. Building a foundation, which includes stability, obedience and the willingness to change, is critical if intimacy with God is to last.

Years ago, I lived in a house that was about eighty years old. It was lovely as long as I didn't go into the basement. When it rained, the basement walls poured out streams of water. Fortunately, the sump pump worked well. I often wondered what structural failure would come next.

Prayer is lifting up your mind and heart to God. Lifting your mind and heart to God is near impossible for you if you are tied to the earth with your brokenness and frailties. Foundations even with one weak brick can weaken the entire structure and eventually will deteriorate other bricks. Intimate prayer requires a sense of unhurried interior quietness, an emptying of your busy thoughts. You have about sixty to eighty thousand thoughts per day. About 70 percent of them are negative. You have roughly three thousand negative thoughts per hour.

Governing your thoughts comes through governing your life. Don't expect much lifting up of anything if you are overwhelmed with a busy life. If you think that you can hurry God to match your schedule, you are mistaken. Praying in a quiet place is not praying in the bathroom. It would be helpful if you had a sacred space in your home.

Often, at intersections, I would wait for an opening in the traffic. I would sit still, pray for patience and wait my turn. Is that prayer? Yes and no. It might just be me reminding myself of a better way to respond to a stressful situation. Does God like these not so great "liftings" of my heart and mind? He most certainly does.

There are all kinds of prayers such as these informal spontaneous prayers. "Help me" is a great prayer. Will these spontaneous prayers advance your relationship with a communicating God? I certainly hope so. You are reminding yourself about your dependency upon God. If God is the initiator, then it follows that He has inspired these prayers.

One afternoon, as I was driving on the expressway, I had a vision. The ground rose up in front of me; the earth surrendered to heaven. God's message was, "Turn your spiritual dial, and you would see that heaven is here. I am always before you." I don't mean to say that earth and heaven are the same. I am saying that if you could just perceive things more clearly, you would become aware of God's presence everywhere. I was somewhat frightened about crashing at seventy miles an hour during the vision. Raising your heart and mind needs to be done in a more conducive place. Of course, that one was on God. He does have a way of being in charge when divine things happen. This is a good point.

You can't force a truly divine, mystical, or godly communication. Our job is to be available. If all you do is pray in your car to and from work, as many people do, or enjoy Christian music while driving and think that satisfies an intimate relationship with your Creator, you are mistaken.

There are other kinds of prayer that do not advance our relationship with a communicating God. A popular prayer could be called "let's make a deal." It is similar to the TV program where the contestants try to negotiate for their own interest. That is fine for a TV program, but it won't work with God.

I remember in my early years, I would frequently promise God that if He gave me such and such, I would do some grand gesture in thanksgiving. Later, I learned that this was witchcraft. If you make terms with God through some manipulation or by promising God something, or by praying in Jesus' name so He would be bound to do what you asked, you are practicing witchcraft, misuse of Scripture, self-absorption and God the genie on the shelf all simultaneously.

When you speak in someone's name, you are speaking on behalf of that person. For example, if I were to ask a monk to give a specific message to another monk, he would be speaking in my name. Praying "in Jesus' name" is saying to God that you know Jesus so well that if Jesus were speaking right now, you know that He would be petitioning for the same thing. That is an awesome responsibility. Do you really know Jesus that well?

There are many ways that you can try to manipulate our dear Lord. One is through excessive ritual. I have seen good hearted Christians abuse rituals by putting confidence in their use as kind of magic. For example, they could have various intentions such as a need for protection. Personally, I would simply ask God to protect me from.... Please remember that the "put a hedge around me" prayer is simply a metaphor.

A local charismatic preacher tried manipulating God by reminding Him how he, the preacher, had been so magnificently grand in his success in doing God's will that God owed him his petition. I can't imagine where the preacher got the idea that being obedient was a savings account that he could draw upon.

Fasting has the potential to be another form of manipulation. For example, fasting to acquire a false sense of righteousness or to increase the building fund could be a form of manipulation. A number of churches promote fasting by the entire congregation for a period of time and for a specific purpose. Fasting during Lent is a great idea. One of the purposes for fasting is to learn how to exercise self-control. Control over food is transferable to other lustful thoughts. The reliable source, Scripture, does encourage fasting. Fasting from food in the Testaments also eliminates an enormous amount of time spent in food preparation. Now more time is available for prayer.

I did a serious fast only two times in my life. The first culminated in a wonderful vision of seeing Christ's resurrection. The power of God's Glory was very moving. The second time, I was busy counseling. The fasting created a sugar drop, dizziness and some confusion. That prevented me from being responsible toward my clients. So I stopped. My old age and potential for diabetes present a situation where I have to be cautious on fasting. No more extreme food fasting for me. Short modest food fasting or fasting from TV, especially the news, or some other activity would be more appropriate. Fasting from food or other things is fine if it is done thoughtfully and with awareness of any medical limitations. As with anything, there are extremes even of seemingly good things. Fasting is not stopping from something that you can't do anyway.

You may have been misinformed regarding praying to the saints. I deeply regret that you are missing out in the participation of what St. Paul calls the Mystical Body of Christ. St. Paul teaches that although we are separate from other believers by their deaths, we can still pray for each other. Petitioning to the saints is not worshiping them. That would be sinful. You would be asking a saint to petition Christ on your behalf. I often pray to St. Benedict to help me with wisdom, strength and to keep me safe from the evil one. St. Benedict and I both know that St. Benedict is not the one directly giving me anything. Rather St. Benedict is petitioning Christ on my behalf.

There is also misinformation on the use of religious articles, such as the crucifix, religious pictures and religious medals. They are legitimate tools to help you stay focused. Often the blessings prayed on the articles will benefit you greatly.

I am concerned that you have been erroneously taught that if you want something, ask God once and then back off. Have faith, don't ask again. That sounds like misplaced faith and a manipulation of our reliable source, Scripture. The story of the woman who persistently petitions to the unjust judge eventually wears him out and he grants her petition. I extrapolate, keep praying and don't give up.

God cannot be manipulated or worn out, but our sincere petitions over a period of time are important to Him and to ourselves. Praying over a period of time gives you the opportunity for clarity as to your real desires. Have you noticed when you originally asked for something, later you changed your mind? The graces that you received even praying for the wrong thing God uses so you might grow in maturity and clarity. That is also true when a large number of people join in prayer.

If you don't have a real desire for your petition, you will stop praying or fasting for it. Now that is clarity. Preferably, you prayed before your petitionary prayer, asking God what you should do regarding your need. Then you wait until He answers. It could take a while before He answers. It is important to know exactly what He wants you to do.

The advantage of having an active prayer life is the certainty that you are walking in, with and through God. Prayer is mostly listening.

- CHAPTER 10 -
REALISTIC EXPECTATIONS

Have you ever attended a motivational meeting and learned ten new bold things? You then go to your office or home and try to suddenly incorporate all ten at the same time? The result is frequently chaos and resistance.

The same goes for prayer and spiritual exercises. Move into your new patterns slowly and thoughtfully and involve those around you. You might even invite them to join you in all or part of your pilgrimage. A husband and wife praying together is a very powerful and bonding experience. It is difficult to develop and sustain a new discipline. There is a normal resistance and difficulties in finding time from the whirlwind of earthly stresses and responsibilities.

That is one of the reasons why people from a variety of Christian backgrounds join our Cistercian Order as monks or oblates. They seek continued guidance and support. A monk or oblate is a seeker who strives to encounter God and seeks a methodology and support to do so. The Rule of St. Benedict has been helpful for over fourteen hundred years.

The first step toward realistic expectations is to go slowly. Balance in your life is important. Having a rule of life, the rule of St. Benedict or making your own rule is essential. Your own rule should state your priorities and methodologies for obtaining your goals. You will get lost without a vision.

When I was a college instructor, the adult students were often overwhelmed with family, work, college studies and who knows what else. Often we had conversations on balance. You can't have everything. Quite un-American to say that, but when you make one choice, it automatically rules out other choices. It really won't be too difficult to find time for prayer if you do so a little at a time.

If you lived in a residential monastery, the prayer routine might be the following:

6:00 am—First Hour (*Matins/Lauds/Orthros*)
9:00 am—Third Hour (*Trece*)
Noon Prayer—Sixth Hour (*Sext*)
3:00 pm—Ninth Hour (*None*)
6:00 pm (*Vespers/Evensong*)
9:00 pm Midnight Prayer (*Compline*)

There would also be time within each day for Lectio Divina and study.

Most monks also work about eight hours a day. There is also eating, some social time and attending to other particular needs. A residential monk is also busy and sometimes is overwhelmed with the whirlwind of life. The advantage for the monks is that they live within a dedicated support group.

You may have difficulty with such a rigid schedule, but you can take five or ten minute breaks throughout the day to pray. There are a wide variety of prayer books and apps that will help you. Short moments of prayer throughout the day can keep God before you and remind you that He is with you always. While short prayers are great, they don't exactly raise your heart and mind to God. It takes more time, more silence and more listening than talking. Prayer is really about listening.

The best way to create a habit of prayer is to do it daily. That hour or two for quiet listening and Lectio Divina may not be available even for the most enthusiastic. You might try setting aside two or three opportunities per week for your longer, quieter prayers.

Never feel guilty if you are not perfectly accomplishing your goals. The criterion is to be sincere and keep pushing forward. Try a different plan. Just keep pushing forward. Certainly ask God for help. Prayer life has ups and downs. The goal is a pilgrimage of learning, listening and being available to God.

I usually get up about 5:00 a.m. I get my coffee and go into my prayer room. Other times, I might go to my chapel. I am fortunate to have several sacred places throughout the monastery. I pray for the Cistercian Order, read the "Office of the Readings" and "Morning Prayer." Most of my prayers are taken from a prayer book called *The Liturgy of the Hours* or sometimes called *Christian Prayer.* I have used this prayer book for over forty years. There are many other prayer books, but I really appreciate this one because each of the seven hours has psalms, Scripture readings, prayers and use the Liturgical seasonal calendar. "The Office of Readings" also has excerpts from the Church Fathers.

Praying or singing the psalms is a wonderful experience. You need not have a "singing voice" or know how to chant. Let your soul create the music.

By praying or reading slowly, certain verses will jump out and seek reflection. One of my favorites is "My soul yearns for you." I often stop, reflect and feel the pain of yearning for God and the joy of finding Him. There will be verses that will become your favorites.

Reading or praying slowly with moments, sometimes rather long moments, of reflection are effectively Lectio Divina. An hour goes by rather quickly. You might want to add another hour of spiritual reading. Spiritual reading should be focused on significant books, not those popular books and pamphlets with someone's emotional often incorrect or misleading, self-absorbed comfort for an emotional need of the moment. The psalms will address whatever you need. Jesus prayed the psalms and the Church has always prayed the same. We need not waste our time reading pop psychology or doing New Age "Centering Prayer." Two hours will pass quickly.

Many people ask how I accomplish so much. They probably say the same about you. Yes, days are busy, but taking a moment here and there to stop and pray is not that difficult. Always walking in gratitude is a big help.

There are times when I will take a "Desert Day." I do nothing other than pray and am quiet. Sometimes I would only take a morning or afternoon, but taking a whole day is really nice. You might have to get out of your home to accomplish a "Desert Day." A getaway might be rather refreshing.

A friend and I email a daily gratitude meditation to each other. That has been a great moment to refocus on what is really important and how God is indeed present every second of every day. It is also a joy to share that gratitude with another.

You may pray before going to bed. An examination of conscience, how much have I sinned today, forgive me, Lord, is a good evening practice. You might end the day with a period of gratitude. Praying with your marriage partner is essential. Praying with your head on the pillow is fine, but remember, snoring is not praying in tongues.

It is possible to create a balance in your life. You will enjoy regular prayer with various lengths of time, a variety of prayers, and Scripture readings. By giving this gift of time to your Lord, it makes you available to listen to Him. When you pray, do not force an emotion, insight or reflection. I try not to expect anything. This is my gift of time to God. Silence is more important than a lot of words. Often the fruits of my prayers come at surprising times of insight, wisdom, courage, boldness and patience.

You can't pretend with God. He already knows what you are trying to hide. That is both scary and comforting. Be transparent with Him. I remember during one morning prayer when I complained to God. I said that I was expecting more peaceful emotions as a fruit of my prayers. I did say that the prayers were helpful but not enough. Fortunately, lightning did not strike me dead! Instead, what I heard was, "Controlling your emotions is not my job, go for a run." I never expected that. I learned that God cares and will help, but there is a whole lot that I can do for myself. Go for a run.

St. Benedict encourages short prayers, a lot of prayers and a lot of quiet. Distractions are normal. They will be frustrating, but remember they are normal. You can simply step back from your prayers for a moment. Breathe. Then go back to prayer. It is okay to get up and walk around. Saying your prayers out loud helps eliminate internal distractions. Be assured that the more you practice, there will be fewer distractions. Environmental distractions are more difficult to control. However, you can choose a quieter time of day and quieter place to pray. Having a sacred place, with a candle, crucifix, holy pictures, etc. will be of great help. Your family will learn to stay away when you are in your sacred place.

Being unhealthy and tired will make it difficult to raise your heart and mind to God. That doesn't mean you shouldn't try. You can just sit there and say, "Here I am, Lord." And be quiet.

Clinical depression, ADHD and just about any disability can make prayer difficult. God knows and understands. Discuss this with your medical professionals. They may be able to help.

Sometimes God will seem far away. That is normal. When you are depressed, worried, anxious and in one of your more broken and fragile moments, God does seem far away. A long positive history of godly intimacy helps you to remember that God is actually all around you whether you realize it or not. Just keep on reading and praying your prayer book.

Your prayer life is a pilgrimage unto itself. Often it begins with excitement as you try new prayer practices. After a while, it might seem as though it is not working and can be very frustrating. Then seemingly out of nowhere, God really shows up, and you get encouraged. This could then be followed by a real emptiness. You might even question the value of all these prayers. Later, you will move out of yourself and become more unified with God, others and the world.

Do not be discouraged. These various experiences are a result of your own brokenness and fragileness. Keep pressing forward with your prayer book and Scripture. It is indeed worth the effort.

You might be misusing the phrase "the dark night of the soul." Only the most holy of persons experience "the dark night of the soul." The experience is a terrible wrenching, emptiness, emotional and sometimes physical pain, dizziness, and so on. It happens because those who really have intimacy with God feel that they have been abandoned. There is often a mixture of despair and hope. The "dark night" can last for a very long time. They have not actually been abandoned. When they finally come "into the Light," they are even closer to God.

What you are most likely experiencing is a spiritual desert. You bring that upon yourself by not resting, sleeping and eating well. Perhaps your prayer life has also suffered. Take a rest. Do something different in your prayer practices and confess your sins, particularly your sins against loved ones.

You may also experience a bit of a torment within yourself and uneasiness with God. That happens when you are in conflict with God's will and you don't want to be submissive. Look at that carefully and confess your sins and submit. I have had moments of interior torment and anguish. Out of nowhere, I cry in grief. My Spiritual Director suggested that I was in a spiritual purge. I was so excited that I said, "God, go for it. Purge away." There are other times that I am filled with overwhelming gratitude and cry in joy. Many times, in the middle of a relaxing evening, I would get overwhelmed for no apparent reason. I know it is God inspired. I look forward to one day understanding.

You might also have had an experience of gaining ground in intimacy with God then, all of a sudden, lose it. That can happen for a number of reasons. The first is when you become closer to God; you realize that He is really far different than what you have been trying to make Him. And so it seems that you or He is farther away. You might ask God why you are resistant to the truth.

The second reason for feeling distant from God is unrepentant serious sin which puts you at odds with God. You are now fodder for Satan. Expect your life to go badly.

There is no unforgivable, confessed, repented sin. Having a Spiritual Director and Confessor is a real benefit in times like this. They can also help you educate your conscience. You are responsible to know what God holds defiant. Lack of that knowledge can also hold you back from intimacy.

Never think that Satan can't get to you. Always be on the watch. Satan can mimic godly experiences. Satan can get you to think that you are a special holy person and rules don't apply to you.

Just being a churchgoer is not enough to protect you from the evil one. You need very close friends who are bold enough to tell you the truth and challenge you to change.

You would be wise to have a Spiritual Director and a Confessor.

A wise pilgrim never travels alone.

- CHAPTER 11 -
TAKE CARE OF YOURSELF

Everything influences everything. If the weather is hot, I am miserable. If it is cold, I am miserable. If I am hungry, I am miserable. If I am too full, I am miserable. Everything affects everything. Your body affects your soul. Your body and soul affect your spirit. You can do things to keep your entire self healthy and strong. Cistercian Monks were the first to understand the interaction between body, soul and spirit.

It you want your spirit to become intimate with God, you have to take your soul and body on the pilgrimage with you. My efforts to describe the purpose of and interaction among your body, soul and spirit will fall short of the totality of the interactions. We are more mystery than science or theology.

I feel that it is necessary to point out that whatever is negative or harmful to humankind is from original sin still operating, the devil, or our personal or corporate sins. God does *not* give, cause, or use evil for His purposes. God does not give us burdens of any kind to test us in any way. Believing otherwise is our misguided way of avoiding responsibility for our own actions. Mostly we experience sowing and reaping. Of course, through grace, we can overcome the consequences of our sowing and reaping.

We often mistake the enthusiasm of young Christians to mean spiritual and or emotional maturity. Those who have been around for a long time sometimes think that just "showing up" actually produces spiritual and emotional maturity. Some mistakenly believe a desire to do good, be good and pray ten minutes a day will actually produce anything other than false pride. God's grace is more like yeast than a lightning bolt. Our pilgrimage is more about the cross than moments of emotional self-satisfaction. The closer we become to God, the more He seems to become unapproachable. The more we actually understand our worthlessness, the more we want to approach Him. Yes, becoming a Christian is more a life journey of dying to self and becoming more intimate with the Divine.

Finally, our walk should lead to a profound understanding that everything is prayer, everything is God and that we live in, with and through Him.

The goal is that you take care of everything that you are.

Body provides a corruptible material vehicle for the soul and spirit and can, with the help of Divine Grace, be drawn to God.

Soul is the non-material and eternal character of the body, e.g., gender, intellect, free will, reason and personality.

Spirit is non-material and eternal. It gives life to the body-soul combination.

The body, soul and spirit are affected by environment, family of origin, the individual's activities, e.g., religion, education and purposeful growth.

It is most helpful to see man as a triune person, meaning each part affects the other in both positive and negative ways. Below is a modest, although hopefully accurate, list of potentially positive and negative effects upon each body, soul and spirit. I will list them in terms of the positive and negative elements acting upon the individual as they approach God in this world.

It is good to note that God can, if we allow Him, overcome all of our obstacles that can come between man and Himself.

Body

Positive effects upon: good mental and physical health, healthy lifestyle, thriving emotional and physical environment, an active spirituality and community life, a healthy soul and spirit.

Negative effects upon: psychiatric problems, lack of emotional stability, chronic illness, physical disabilities, diseases, destructive emotional or physical environment, little or no spirituality, and minimal or no community involvement.

Soul

Positive effects upon: Include here the positive effects of the body as seen above. Additionally, you might add education, purposeful emotional and spiritual growth, participation in a church, and social structure. The positive development of conscience, healthy, intimate, and corporate relationships, a good sense of self including sexuality, problem-solving, the ability to understand and appreciate non-material things such as ideas, music, the arts. This individual is more heavenly bound.

Negative effects upon: Include here the negative effect on the body as seen above. Additionally, you might add erroneous education, no or little emotional and spiritual growth, and little or no participation in a church and social activities. Improper or no development of conscience, no healthy, intimate, and corporate relationships, no or little healthy sense of self including sexuality, weak problem-solving skills, little or no understanding or appreciation of non-material things such as ideas, music, the arts. This individual is more earthly bound.

Spirit

Positive effects upon: Include here the positive effects upon both the body and soul. The following helps the spirit to grow and produce more life to the individual. For this person, everything is spiritual, everything is prayer and everything is God. There is a focus on serving others, humility, meekness and exhibiting the fruits and gifts of the Holy Spirit. This individual has an investment in prayer, reception of the Sacraments, church life, a Rule of Life, a spiritual director and a confessor. This person studies the church fathers, history and is a seeker of truth.

Negative effects upon: Include here the negative effects upon both the body and soul. The following hurts the spirit to grow and produce more life to the individual. For this person, everything is about him or herself, what he or she can possess, personal power, emphasis on negative feelings, self-esteem and status. There is little or no focus on serving others unless there is something in it for him or her, and even at the expense of another's reputations. This individual believes that he or she is the judge on truth and will not submit to authority.

- CHAPTER 12 -
SPIRITUAL DIRECTION AND RECONCILIATION

Spiritual Direction

Christianity is a community experience. We are intentioned to find God by participating in a faith community. Some of the gifts that are available within a community are spiritual direction and reconciliation with God. Spiritual direction is concerned with helping a person directly with his or her relationship with God. The underlying question is, "Who is God for me, and who am I for Him?" Spiritual direction transcends any particular jurisdiction or denomination.

The Director helps the person to address God directly and to listen to what God has to communicate. The focus of this kind of direction is the relationship between God and the person. The person is helped not so much to understand the relationship better but to engage in it and to enter into dialogue with God. Spiritual direction of this kind focuses on what happens when a person listens to and responds to a self-communicating God.

We define spiritual direction as help given by a director that enables a person to pay attention to God's personal communication, to respond and grow in intimacy with this God and to live out the consequences of the relationship both personally and in community. The focus on this type of direction is on experience, not ideas, and specifically on religious experience.

The spiritual director is most interested in what happens when a person consciously puts himself into the presence of God. Not that the director has little or no interest in the rest of a person's life. He is interested in the whole person, but the focus of interest is the prayer experience.

Although spiritual direction is best done in the presence of the Director, it may be done by video conferencing.

Reconciliation/Confession

Those who approach the Sacrament of Reconciliation obtain pardon and absolution for the offenses committed against God and is, at the same time, reconciled to the Church which they have wounded by their sins. Private, auricular confession is preferred over communal penitential rites.

Every Christian can go to God directly for forgiveness and should do so daily. There are times, however, when the penitent yearns to hear the words of forgiveness from someone with the authority to do so. Jesus knew our needs and gave the Church via its bishops and priests the authority to absolve sin in His name.

Male bishops and priests are the sole ministers of the sacrament. The Seal of the Confession is *absolute*. The contents and identity of a penitent can never be made known under any circumstances. The sacrament must be readily available to anyone who reasonably asks for it. The confessor may refuse to hear a confession or give absolution if the penitent does not come to the sacrament with the intent and willingness to be reconciled and amended.

The Sacrament of Reconciliation can only be administered to one person at a time, and they and the Confessor must be present to each other. It cannot be done over the phone or video conference. The Sacrament of Reconciliation normally contains spiritual counsel by the confessor. The sacrament may be administered in any suitable location.

Protestant churches do not offer sacramental reconciliation but do have available penitential services with assurances from Scripture that a sincerely contrite person is forgiven.

- CHAPTER 13 -
THREE EXERCISES IN MEDITATION AND PRAYER

Your pilgrimage has so far helped you to get over yourself, pull out those tangled roots and build a foundation. These three meditations and prayer exercises will bring your earlier reflection skills to a deeper level. In previous chapters I had provided an open ended reflection on trust and a series of questions as a format for your chapter reflections with an opportunity for you to create a prayer.

These articles can go much deeper than simply information. I would like you to read them over several times. The articles are short and highly focused. Meditate on them. Ask your own questions and listen for revelations. Discover your strengths and weaknesses. Listen carefully. Where is the Holy Spirit leading you?

Ask the Holy Spirit to help you develop a significantly moving prayer.

1. Listen with the Ear of Your Heart

"Can you hear me now? Can you hear me now?" The narrator repeats the question over and over throughout the popular commercial. This is an interesting phrase that both markets his product and mirrors your personal need to be heard.

You need to be heard. You don't necessarily have to agree or support me, but please, please hear me. When you hear me, I am validated. I become a person of some value. To be validated, you will talk on the cell phone about trivial nonsense, chatter all day about nothing important to anyone who will listen or even create an argument to get attention. This is a sad state of affairs to be sure.

Let us speak about listening skills. You can recall what you know about listening skills by remembering what Mama told you, "You have two ears and one mouth, so listen more than you speak." Actually the 90/10 rule came from this. That is to listen 90 percent of the time and speak only 10 percent. It sure would be a quieter planet.

Active listening means full participation by the listener and response to the speaker. This might include such communication efforts as mirroring. Mirroring is speaking back what you have just heard.

Passive listening is thinking of your response rather than really listening. You could also be viewing a sports channel, reading the paper or almost anything other than listening. Basically, you are not really present to the speaker and show little interest in what is being said.

The next level of listening skills is to listen with the ear of your heart. At first, that may seem an unusual statement. But slow down for a moment and listen to the words: listen with the ear of your heart. I think you will figure it out. Listen in such a way that the speaker, or writer, moves you toward transformation.

Imagine listening to your mate complain about his day. Imagine moving to the ear of your heart and the effect his words of sorrow, conflict, stress and failure have on your heart. Your response to him would be different than if you just simply heard the words. You would be transformed, moved, more charitable and compassionate.

The heart needs you to speak slowly. Look at your beloved. Do not be in a rush. Save your important messages for a time when you are together. Do not discuss them over the cell phone. Touch them whenever something is really important to you. Speak softly. The heart is tender. It gets frightened when you are loud, critical or sarcastic. Be careful with your words. Say what you really mean. Be clear and precise. Do not continually repeat yourself. The heart hears better with fewer words.

It takes practice to listen with the ear of your heart. You need to develop a quiet spirit. The quiet spirit is developed through a desire to be present to your beloved. Spend time in quiet. Let there be no noise, no distractions. Listen to yourself. Still your body. Move slowly. Don't always be involved with movement. When you listen, your goal is to be in empathic union with the speaker. Look into their eyes. Give them your understanding and respond with few words, a smile or tear. Mostly be with them.

2. Prayer is the work of God

All too often, I hear people complain about dryness in prayer. They complain from an erroneous belief that prayer was intended to always be fulfilling and meaningful. St. John of the Cross calls this spiritual gluttony.

I remember reading a letter between St. Teresa of Avila and St. John of the Cross. She was encouraging him to join her on a trip to see the latest fad in miracles. He responded that there were enough miracles in his garden so he would not go. Let me assure you that prayer is mostly an act of obedience and a joyful giving of our time and self to the Lord. When I pray, I am giving my gift, self-oblation of time, to my Creator. He is not obliged to respond in any way. When He does respond, it is mostly through enlightenment or a better understanding.

I find God the most during the Eucharist. I "saw" the bread turn into flesh. Frequently, I feel joined with the saints. I also become one with the Lord when I pray with others. He often directs my prayers and brings healing.

Br. Brendan, OCCO, reported seeing me transcend during prayer. So, dear ones, prayer can be very exciting at times. God will create those moments. Meanwhile, simply do the work of God.

3. Gratitude

Gratitude keeps us alive and kicking. The lack of gratitude makes us self-absorbed and lifeless. I tend to think that when Eve said to Adam, "Try this one," if they had stopped for a moment and had spoken words of thanks to the Lord for all He had given to them, everything would have been different.

Gratitude changes us. We get happier, more empowered, more creative, more emotionally secure and more of the good things. Gratitude will open our souls to the unity of God, self and others. Gratitude moves us from limitations and fear to expansion and love.

- CHAPTER 14 -
LIST OF PRAYER BOOKS AND APPS

Several options exist to facilitate the offering of the Liturgy of the Hours. Some are simplistic and some are quite expansive. The following list represents various texts that you might consider when selecting a book for daily prayer.

Simple Options for the Beginner

Give Us This Day
https://giveusthisday.org

This text presents a simplified form of daily prayer that follows the rhythm of traditional prayer but in a more compact form. It also includes the readings for daily Mass. This format is perfect for someone new to daily prayer or for individuals reconnecting to the practice after a long time away. This text is purchased as a monthly subscription, which can be pricey, but it has the virtue of laying the entire prayer office out for you. Liturgical Press makes a sample available through the website noted above. At times, the reflection breakouts can trend toward an emphasis on applied Christianity, which means if you are looking for high theological reflection in your daily prayer, it may not suit your needs. Though published by a Roman Catholic monastic order, the text is presented in such a way that is broadly ecumenical.

Magnificat
https://us.magnificat.net

This text presents a simplified form of daily prayer that follows the rhythm of traditional prayer, but in a

105

more compact form. It also includes the readings for daily Mass. This format is perfect for someone new to daily prayer or for individuals reconnecting to the practice after a long time away. This text is purchased as a monthly subscription, which can be pricey, but it has the virtue of laying the entire prayer office out for you. The publisher makes a sample issue available through the website noted above. At times, the reflection breakouts can trend toward an emphasis on dogmatic Christianity, which means if you are looking for application-based reflections in your daily prayer; it may not suit your needs. The text is thoroughly Roman Catholic, which means that, at times, some individuals from other traditions may have to adapt some of the prayer texts on the fly to suit their needs.

The Glenstal Book of Daily Prayer
https://www.amazon.com/Glenstal-Book-Daily-Prayer-Benedictine/dp/0814632734/ref=sr_1_3

Published by a Benedictine abbey, this simple, accessible book of prayer will give users the rhythm of daily prayer in easy-to-digest and simple forms. It is an ideal introduction to fixed-hour prayer, but those who have a history with this type of prayer may find the two-week cycle through much of the year to be limiting. A wonderful resource to accompany the use of this book is the *Glenstal Book of Readings for the Season*, which provides enriching devotional additions for the festal seasons of the Church Year.

Intermediate Options

Trinity Daily Prayer
https://thetrinitymission.org

This text, mostly available online (but print editions are generally available, consult the website), is pretty straightforward but contains expanded content (longer readings, intercessions, and prayer texts) than the simpler forms. It is published by a conservative Anglican body and contains only the texts of the prayer offices and the readings, no reflections. *Trinity Daily Prayer* offers three texts daily morning, midday, and evening.

A Book of Daily Prayer (Two Volumes)
Volume I: http://www.lulu.com/shop/robert-lyons/a-book-of-daily-prayer-volume-i/hardcover/product-24316127.html

Volume II: http://www.lulu.com/shop/robert-lyons/a-book-of-daily-prayer-volume-ii/hardcover/product-24254170.html

This text, published in two volumes for ease of use, lays out each day's office in full but does require you to keep an eye on a calendar to know which choices to make on what days. Sundays and Holy Days are given a lengthier text, while ordinary weekdays and Saturdays are given a somewhat briefer text. This is intended to balance the everyday responsibilities of believers with the sanctification of time and those days that carry a particular meaning in the Christian tradition.

Volume I covers Advent, Lent, Holy Week, and the Easter Seasons, while Volume II covers the remainder of the year. Individuals desiring to incorporate a reflection into their prayers will need to select their own text to accomplish this.

Daily Office Book (Two-Volume Set)
https://www.amazon.com/Daily-Office-Book-Two-Set/ dp/0898691397

This text, first published in the 1980s, provides two small pocket-sized books, one for each year of the Episcopal/Lutheran Daily Office Lectionary. They allow for traditional or contemporary language prayer, though the psalms and readings are in the 79 BCP and RSV translations respectively. It has a cousin, the *Contemporary Office Book*, which is a single volume with contemporary language that uses the NRSV as the biblical text. Both are relatively easy to use, provided you use the regular thirty-day Anglican cycle of psalms.

For All the Saints (Four-Volume Set)
http://alpb.org/books/for-all-the-saints-a-prayer-book-for-and-by- the-church/

An outstanding, thorough, yet easily usable text, this Lutheran Breviary provides three Scripture readings daily and a reading from a theologian, Church Father, or other notable Christian so that one could use two readings at each of the major offices (morning and evening prayer). The four volumes cover two years and are fairly easy to get the hang of within a few weeks of usage. The Psalter is that of the *Lutheran Book of Worship*, which is substantially that of the 1979 BCP, and the Bible translation is RSV.

Advanced Options

Christian Prayer and *Liturgy of the Hours* (Four-Volume Set) *Christian Prayer:*
https://www.amazon.com/Christian-Prayer-Catholic-Book-Publishing/dp/0899424066

Liturgy of the Hours:
https://www.amazon.com/Liturgy-Hours-Catholic-Book-Publishing/dp/0899424090/ref=sr_1_1

These are relatively complex texts which represent the official Roman Catholic version of the Hours. The four-volume *Liturgy of the Hours* set is the most comprehensive and is the best investment in this line for an individual seriously dedicated to the work of daily prayer. *Christian Prayer* condenses the material down to one volume and omits all but a shell of the Office of Readings (where the bulk of Scripture and Patristic Reflections are found) but does make the text more accessible. There is a third book, *Shorter Christian Prayer,* that boils down the material in *Christian Prayer* even further but which is still complex in its own right.

It should be noted that there is a website, *Universalis,* that provides the current Roman Catholic Liturgy of the Hours fully populated and ready to go for those who wish to pray in an electronic format. They offer an app for IOS and Android that allows you to download to your phone as well.

Benedictine Daily Prayer: A Short Breviary (Second Edition)
https://www.amazon.com/Benedictine-Daily-Prayer-Short-20Breviary/dp/0814637027/ref=sr_1_1

This text, published by the Benedictine Monks of Saint John's Abbey in Collegeville, Minnesota, is an improvement on the first edition but has a steep learning curve. Don't let the advertising slogan "pray in a simpler way" fool you this is a Breviary you do have to work with. It has the virtue of being somewhat flexible once you get to know your way around it and has a Benedictine spirituality at its core.

Apps

There are a number of excellent apps for your digital devices that will be of help: "Breviary Tunes," "Divine Office," "IBreviary," "Laudate," "Daily TV Mass." If you go to "Book of Common Prayer" in your app store there are a large number of options. Certainly, if any app will complement your spiritual direction, try it out.

Prayer book list was developed by Father Robert Lyons, M.Div., BCC, CPES.

- CHAPTER 15 -
TYPES OF PRAYER

You have been discovering that prayer can come in many forms and styles, often beautifully blended.

Blessing and Adoration

Adoration is the attitude of man acknowledging that he is a creature before his Creator. It exalts the greatness of the Lord who made us and the almighty power of the Savior who sets us free from evil. Adoration is homage of the spirit to the King of Glory and respectful silence in the presence of the ever greater God.

Prayer of Petition

Christian petition is centered on the desire and search for the Kingdom to come in keeping with the teaching of Christ. There is a hierarchy in these petitions. We pray first for the Kingdom, then for what is necessary to welcome it and cooperate with its coming.

When we share in God's saving love, we understand that every need can become the object of petition. Christ, who assumed all things in order to redeem all things, is glorified by what we ask the Father in His name. It is with this confidence that St. James and St. Paul exhort us to pray at all times.

Prayer of Intercession

Intercession is a prayer of petition that leads us to pray as Jesus did. He is the one intercessor with the Father on behalf of all men, especially sinners. He is "able for all time to save those who draw near to God through him, since he always lives to make intercession for them." The Holy Spirit "himself intercedes for us...and intercedes for the saints according to the will of God."

During the intercession prayer, he who prays looks "not only to his own interests, but also to the interests of others," even to the point of praying for those who do him harm.

Prayer of Thanksgiving

As in the prayer of petition, every event and need can become an offering of thanksgiving. The letters of St. Paul often begin and end with thanksgiving, and the Lord Jesus is always present in it: "Give thanks in all circumstances; for this is the will of God in Christ Jesus for you"; "Continue steadfastly in prayer, being watchful in it with thanksgiving."

Prayer of Praise

Praise is the form of prayer that recognizes most immediately that God is God. It lauds God for His own sake and gives Him glory, quite beyond what He does, but simply because *He is*. It shares in the blessed happiness of the pure of heart who love God in faith before seeing Him in glory. By praise, the Spirit is joined to our spirits to bear witness that we are children of God, testifying to the only Son in whom we are adopted and by whom we glorify the Father. Praise embraces the other forms of prayer and carries them toward him who is its source and goal: the "one God, the Father, from whom are all things and for whom we exist."

The definitions of the five types of prayer have been edited from the *Catechism of the Catholic Church.*

- CHAPTER 16 -
LECTIO DIVINA

You have "pilgrimed" well. Now you can realize the fruits of getting over yourself, pulling up the tangled roots of deeply held erroneous beliefs and building a solid foundation. You are now tilling the soil of your pilgrimage.

Prayer, the raising of your heart and mind to God, cannot be taught because it does not involve a set of skills. Divine intimacy requires putting aside all that you think you know. Prayer requires discipline, asceticism, purification and self-control. Those qualities emerge when you earnestly do the pilgrimage as described in this book.

Reluctance to set a structure and schedule to pray is reflective of your resistance to God. You still do not trust Him. You prefer to withhold yourself and not be led by God.

The discipline of Lectio Divina is a well-founded vehicle that enables you to seek God. Lectio Divina means reading something holy. The reading is thoughtfully done, unlike reading a newspaper. Read very slowly, letting each word, each character speak to you. You may want to study secondary readings to better know the contents of the passage. You are not attempting to be a biblical scholar. Just let the short passage speak to you.

Lectio Divina is meant to go slowly. Stay with each of the following steps until the Lord inspires you to move to the next step. You could possibly spend a week, a month or more on each step. When I first began doing Lectio Divina, the Lord gave me for eight years three simple words, "in the beginning."

When I look back on those eight years, those three words were life-sustaining.

1. **Lectio** means reading. I have included several Lectio Divinas with questions for meditation to help you to get started. When you are ready to go on your own, let God choose what your reading should be. It is okay if it takes you some time to understand where He is leading you. Remember, He initiates everything.

2. **Meditatio** means meditation. While reading your short Scriptural passage, certain ideas or questions may come to mind. Write them down. These ideas may or may not have a direct connection to the reading.

   The Lectio Divinas that are included in this book have some questions listed to give you a helping hand. Those questions may not be the end of the meditation. God might want you to go further. Since you are not in a rush, take your time and let the Holy Spirit lead.

3. **Oratio** means prayer. After a period of meditation, the Holy Spirit will impress upon you certain significant ideas. It may take some time for you to be aware if which items are most important. That is okay. Keep meditating and asking God questions.

   Let God direct your prayers. For example, He might lead you to pray concerning your fear of failure. Your simple prayer might be, "Lord, help me. I am terribly frightful of failure."

4. **Contempatio** means contemplation. This is your holy moment when you turn your prayer over to God. Be quiet. Let God do the work. Do not expect anything or have an agenda.

It is difficult to remain quiet for any length of time. When your mind wanders, bring it back. Have something to focus on like a crucifix. Your contemplation may be relatively short. Come back to it sometime later. This is a slow experience worthy of investment.

Silence requires you to put away your selfish efforts to control and receive rewards or satisfactions. Contemplation is the ultimate expression of trust. Contemplation is a grace given by God. There is nothing that you can do to make contemplation happen other than be still and be willing to be led by God.

The true contemplative's prayer is simply, "Here I am, Lord. Do with me what You will."

- CHAPTER 17 -
LECTIO DIVINAS ON TRUST
AND SELF-DISCOVERY

Trust is a central theme of this book. You have been doing some work regarding trust by utilizing the chapter reflections. This Lectio Divina on trust will pull together your current work and fill in some of the blanks to create a total picture and some healing insightful moments.

This information will teach you how to do the prayer process called Lectio Divina. In this experience of Lectio Divina, we will examine each character and event in a Scripture story and allow the Holy Spirit to help us examine and transform ourselves.

The process of Lectio Divina: (1) Read over the Scripture and know its content well. (2) Meditate on the content and allow yourself to be led by the Holy Spirit. I have included some meditation questions to aid you in this prayer. (3) The Holy Spirit will draw your attention to specific items. Pay close attention to His leading.

(4) Pray sincerely for the healing that the Holy Spirit is leading. (5) Contemplate, be silent, and allow the Holy Spirit to transform you. This process is done slowly and best to be thought more as yeast for the soul than as a microwave for a quick fix. Below is a list of reflective questions. Look deep within yourself and ask the Holy Spirit to inspire, direct and heal you. Ask Him how this Scripture applies to your life. Answer each question completely and honestly. Write down your observations and insights. These reflections will use Scripture in the manner of Lectio Divina, or Divine Reading. Take your time do not rush it through. Use a separate sheet of paper to write your reflections.

Trust and Trusting Lectio Divina

These themes will be included in the Lectio Divina prayer.

Problems with trusting: If your childhood caregivers were inconsistent, emotionally unavailable or rejecting, shame may have been created in you. Shame is the belief that something is fundamentally wrong with you. Some people hold on to negative emotions because they believe that they give them comfort or power. If you are not trustworthy, you would tend to see God and others as not trustworthy.

Trust is established within a relationship when time has been spent assessing the relationship through personal disclosure, sacrificing one's wants for the other's needs, giving time and attention to the other, introspection on your own trustworthiness and whether you trust your own decisions. Do you learn from your errors? Are you willing to risk and be future thinking? Leaving the past behind is important. It is necessary to be a forgiving person and learn to see people and situations as God does.

Things to consider:

You cannot trust others unless you first trust God.

There are levels of trust. For example, you would trust your gardener less than you would your marriage partner.

Does the person you are attempting to trust have the ability and intention to be faithful to their promises? Are they worthy of trust? A sociopath or narcissist does not have the ability to be trustworthy.

Love and trust do not necessarily go together. We are called to love everyone but be very careful whom we trust. It is necessary to forgive before you can trust.

This Scripture came to mind:

> "Create a clean heart in me, O, God, and
> put a new and steadfast spirit within me.
> Turn away your face from my sins, O, God,
> and blot out all my guilt."

I hope this will be a growth filled experience for you and that you will grow in trust toward God the Father and others.

Some things to remember about Mary and Joseph

Mary was about fourteen years old at the time of the Annunciation. Although of young age to our standards, she was raised in the Temple by the High Priest named Joachim and her mother named Anna. Mary was well-educated in both spiritual and temporal matters. Both of her parents were of advanced age and childless. Mary was conceived due to her parents' trusting prayers. In our contemporary terms, Mary was a preacher's kid, a PK. There is every indication that she was raised in an emotionally and spiritually healthy environment and was fervent in her Jewish faith.

Joseph was likely considerably older than Mary. He was thought of in his community as a mature, educated and spiritually sound individual. He was an established carpenter. He was selected to be Mary's husband according to the method of his times. There are stories of a Divine intervention on his behalf.

Joseph and Mary were engaged at the time of the Annunciation, not married, and were not living together and were not sexually active. Engagement was a status held much more seriously than we hold it today. Most believe that Joseph married Mary soon after she told him of her pregnancy. He had the option not to marry her. He could have banished her or had her killed for being pregnant out of wedlock.

We will use these Scriptures for the meditations.

Mary Accepts God's Invitation to Give Birth to, and Mother, Jesus

> In the sixth month of Elizabeth's pregnancy, God sent the angel Gabriel to Nazareth, a town in Galilee to a virgin pledged to be married to a man named Joseph, a descendant of David. The virgin's name was Mary. The angel went to her and said, "Greetings, you who are highly favored! The Lord is with you."
>
> Mary was greatly troubled at his words and wondered what kind of greeting this might be. But the angel said to her, "Do not be afraid, Mary; you have found favor with God. You will conceive and give birth to a son, and you are to call him Jesus. He will be great and will be called the Son of the Most High. The Lord God will give him the throne of his father David, and he will reign over Jacob's descendants forever; his kingdom will never end."
>
> "How will this be," Mary asked the angel, "since I am a virgin?"
>
> The angel answered, "The Holy Spirit will come upon you, and the power of the Most High will overshadow you. So the holy one to be born will be called the Son of God.
>
> Even Elizabeth your relative is going to have a child in her old age, and she who was

said to be unable to conceive is in her sixth month. For no word from God will ever fail."

"I am the Lord's servant," Mary answered. "May your word to me be fulfilled." Then the angel left her. (Luke 1:26–38, NIV)

Joseph Accepts Jesus as His Son

This is how the birth of Jesus the Messiah came about: His mother Mary was pledged to be married to Joseph, but before they came together, she was found to be pregnant through the Holy Spirit. Because Joseph her husband was faithful to the law, and yet did not want to expose her to public disgrace, he had in mind to divorce her quietly.

But after he had considered this, an angel of the Lord appeared to him in a dream and said, "Joseph son of David, do not be afraid to take Mary home as your wife, because what is conceived in her is from the Holy Spirit. She will give birth to a son, and you are to give him the name Jesus, because he will save his people from their sins."

All this took place to fulfill what the Lord had said through the prophet: "The virgin will conceive and give birth to a son, and they will call him Immanuel" (which means "God with us").

When Joseph woke up, he did what the angel of the Lord had commanded him and took Mary home as his wife. But he did not consummate their marriage until she gave birth to a son. And he gave him the name Jesus. (Matthew 1:18–25)

Week 1

Scripture: "In the sixth month of Elizabeth's pregnancy, God sent the angel Gabriel to Nazareth, a town in Galilee, to a virgin pledged to be married to a man named Joseph, a descendant of David. The virgin's name was Mary."

Reflection questions to be answered:

What do you imagine was going through Mary's mind when she experienced this?

What do I know about the person of Mary? Where did she come from? What was her developmental background?

What do I know about me? Where did I come from? What is my developmental background? Did I come from a family that gave their love inconsistently? Were my parents emotionally available? As a child, did I feel accepted?

How does my adult self give and receive love? Am I worthy of trust? Do I say what I mean? Do I learn from my errors/sins? Do I disclose myself to others? Do I generously give my time to others? Do I sacrifice my wants for the needs of others? Do I hold grudges? Do I forgive easily? Am I open and flexible or rigid in my relationships? How would my friends describe me?

Week 2

Scripture: "The angel went to her and said, "Greetings, you who are highly favored! The Lord is with you."

Reflection questions to be answered:

What do you imagine was going through Mary's mind when she heard this?

What words would God use to describe you? Would He say to you, "Well done, good and faithful servant"?

If I relate to Jesus at all, it is from a distance. I believe in my head but not my heart.

I sometimes look to Jesus to be my savior, helper, sustainer, but I doubt if He really cares enough about me personally. Hell feels closer to me than heaven.

Jesus could not forgive my sins. They are too many and too big.

Although I speak all the right words about Jesus and my relationship with Him, I do not really trust Him. I avoid His lordship over my life. I have to be in charge of my life.

God the Father and the Holy Spirit are intellectual concepts and are not realities that dynamically affect my life.

I am afraid to trust. No one, even the Divine, is trustworthy. My whole life has validated this. I know this to be true. I am wired not to believe.

I often want to believe. Honestly, I am riding on the faith of others and what I read. Although again, being honest, I do not read much. Certainly, I do not read Scripture much or go to church much, or even pray much. If I give five minutes a day to God, He is lucky. My laziness and lame excuses of being so busy are really evidence that I do not believe that Jesus is close to me, cares about me, and can affect me in a positive way. Let's be honest, I am more about myself than Jesus.

Week 3

Scripture: "Mary was greatly troubled at his words and wondered what kind of greeting this might be. But the angel said to her, "Do not be afraid, Mary; you have found favor with God."

Reflection questions to be answered:

What do you imagine was going through Mary's mind when she heard this?

What troubles you? What are you afraid of? What do you worry about? How controlling are you? What would your friends say about you in regards to these questions?

When you feel powerless, how do you get your power back? What are your principal emotional resources, e.g., your checkbook, your employment, your social status?

Do you know God the Father I am not referring to the person of Jesus but God the Father well enough to feel favored by Him? Reflect on your favored status or lack thereof.

Week 4

Scripture: "You will conceive and give birth to a son, and you are to call him Jesus. He will be great and will be called the Son of the Most High."

Reflection questions to be answered:

What do you imagine was going through Mary's mind when she heard this?

Has God ever asked you to do something absolutely incredible? If He has not, why do you think that you have not been asked? If you were asked, what was your response? Could God trust you do something *really* important? Why could He trust you or not trust you? What do your answers to these questions mean and how does this affect you?

If God were to ask you to go to Africa to be a missionary, what would you do?

Week 5

Scripture: "How will this be," Mary asked the angel, "since I am a virgin?"

Reflection questions to be answered:

What do you imagine was going through Mary's mind when she heard this? Was she doubting, not trusting God or perhaps merely asking a biological question?

If it were you, what would you ask the angel? Would it be something like, "Yah, sure." "How are you going to do that?" "You're kidding!"

Or might it go something like this: "I want to trust You, Lord, but if I do, what are You going to do to me? I want to be in charge of something here. Wait a moment. Me, pregnant, that is too much. How about something more realistic or something not so difficult. You know, Lord, that I am busy and have other responsibilities. What, me, risk? I haven't done so well in keeping promises in the past, how can I do such a big thing now?"

Week 6

Scripture: "The angel answered, 'The Holy Spirit will come on you, and the power of the Most High will overshadow you. So the holy one to be born will be called the Son of God.'"

Reflection questions to be answered:

What do you imagine was going through Mary's mind when she heard this?

What would be going through your mind if you were told this? Have you ever been told by God that the answers to your questions are mystical, not of this earth, or just plain do not make sense? What was your reply at that time to what He told you?

Do you trust God to be faithful to what He has said in Scripture? Is God truly able to keep His promises? Does He have the ability and intention to do what He has said He would do?

Now if you answered yes to the above, what are your answers to the following:

1. God has commanded you to worship Him every Sunday. What have you done?
2. He has commanded you to refrain from sex prior to marriage. What have you done?
3. God has commanded you to honor your parents. What have you done?
4. God has commanded you to obey all lawful authority. What have you done?

In light of the above questions and reflections, are you a person that could be trusted? Can imperfect people be trusted? What conclusion can you honestly come to in regards to truly trusting God? Is God not trustworthy or are you not trustworthy? Do you have a need for forgiveness? Do you trust God to forgive you? What has God said about forgiveness?

Week 7

Scripture: "Even Elizabeth your relative is going to have a child in her old age, and she who was said to be unable to conceive is in her sixth month. For no word from God will ever fail."

Reflection questions to be answered:

What do you imagine was going through Mary's mind when she heard this?

Special note: Let me remind you that Mary asked, "How can this be?" In an effort to understand, Mary asked so that she could cooperate. Secondly, she did not ask for proof. In your Scripture reading we see that the angel offered proof. God has offered proof throughout Scripture, and when someone demanded proof, things went badly for them.

Having said the above, have you asked for proof of God's will for you? "Give me a sign, Lord?" Why did you require proof or a sign from the Almighty? Are you mightier than He? Is this an effort to control what happens to you if you were to say yes? Do I have a good reason to trust God the Father? Do I need to trust God before I can deeply trust any person?

This is a particularly interesting proof for Mary. Elizabeth's situation since it is similar to her parents' as they waited in old age for the birth of Mary. Do you frequently reflect on God's action in your life past and present? Does it bring you comfort or anxiety? Does God really want to be involved with you and the development of your life? Give examples how He has been intimately close to you. If you cannot give a list, why not?

Week 8

Scripture: "I am the Lord's servant," Mary answered. "May your word to me be fulfilled." Then the angel left her.

Reflection questions to be answered:

What do you imagine was going through Mary's mind when she said this?

Considering the scope of this narrative, Mary is quietly humble at the announcement and quickly submits. Her submission is as a servant.

If God the Father told you that He highly favored you and that you were to do something that would change everything for all time, how would you respond? Some people might broadcast the news to everyone they knew, saying, "God told me that..." Or perhaps even use those words to validate their own opinions. Is that a trustworthy behavior?

How have you been a good servant to the Lord? Give some examples. Would you prefer to see God the Father as friend or Master? Why? Is it easier to relate to Jesus than to God the Father? Why? Can you trust Jesus more easily than His Father? Why?

Week 9

Scripture: "This is how the birth of Jesus the Messiah came about His mother Mary was pledged to be married to Joseph, but before they came together, she was found to be pregnant through the Holy Spirit. Because Joseph her husband was faithful to the law, and ye] did not want to expose her to public disgrace, he had in mind to divorce her quietly."

Reflection questions to be answered:

What do you imagine was going through Joseph's mind when Mary told him of her pregnancy?

Joseph was a man of the law and was passionately in love with Mary. How do you reconcile what is right, the law, with what is merciful? Do you think that Joseph had a difficult time believing Mary's story? Did he have to forgive her? What for?

Mary took an action that would affect Joseph without first giving him the opportunity to voice his consent. Was this fair? Do you think this was an act of trust on Mary's part? Trust in whom?

When someone changes your life without your consent, what do you do? Can that be an act of trust in them, believing that it is for your best interest, or does it seem like an intrusion into your freedoms? Where is servanthood in this matter?

It seems that Joseph spent considerable time thinking about Mary's best interests rather than his hurt and self-interest. When someone offends you, what do you do? Is that a trustworthy behavior?

Week 10

Scripture: "But after he had considered this..."

Reflection questions to be answered:

What do you imagine was going through Joseph's mind when he considered his options and feelings? Do you think that Joseph remembered the good times with Mary, including her personal relationship with God, her family and community? Did Joseph believe that Mary was a trustworthy person? How might that have contributed to his considerations?

What goes through your mind when someone offends you or breaks the trust? Is it more about you than them? Are you caught up in revenge, threats of leaving, holding on to anger, using the event as a method of gaining power over the other? Do you remind yourself of how the other has sacrificed for you in the past and the goodness of their character? Do you focus on forgiveness? Is forgiveness necessary for trust to be reestablished? Do you focus on the future of the relationship rather than on the hurtful event in the past? Have you broken the trust of your promises with the person who has offended you by holding on to your pain and not doing every merciful thing you can?

Week 11

Scripture: "But after he had considered this, an angel of the Lord appeared to him in a dream and said, 'Joseph son of David, do not be afraid to take Mary home as your wife, because what is conceived in her is from the Holy Spirit. She will give birth to a son, and you are to give him the name Jesus because he will save his people from their sins.'"

"All this took place to fulfill what the Lord had said through the prophet: 'The virgin will conceive and give birth to a son, and they will call him Immanuel (which means God with us).'"

"When Joseph woke up, he did what the angel of the Lord had commanded him and took Mary home as his wife. But he did not consummate their marriage until she gave birth to a son. And he gave him the name Jesus."

Reflection questions to be answered:

What kind of emotional or spiritual movement did Joseph have to go through to come to be able to hear the Lord?

What kind of changes do you have to make to not only accept and forgive but to move into a new and better relationship with someone who has offended you? The essence of reconciliation is not just forgiveness, rebuilding the trust, but an all-out effort to build a new and better relationship with the offender.

Joseph took Mary back not on condition, not where he had to monitor her future behaviors, but a total lifelong absolute commitment of husband to a wife.

Can you do the same? Why? Why not? What is pressing you forward? What is holding you back? Are you opening yourself up to hearing from God and receiving His grace to trust in Him to trust in each other? If you are not willing to do that, what are your options?

Self-Discovery, Lectio Divina

This is an important Lectio Divina for anyone who is seriously seeking to better understand themselves.

This information will teach you how to do the prayer process called Lectio Divina. In this experience of Lectio Divina, we will examine each character and event in this Scripture story and allow the Holy Spirit to help us examine and transform ourselves.

The process of Lectio Divina: (1) Read over the Scripture and know its content well. (2) Meditate on the content and allow yourself to be led by the Holy Spirit. I have included some meditation questions to aid you in this prayer. (3) The Holy Spirit will draw your attention to specific items. Pay close attention to His leading. (4) Pray sincerely for the healing that the Holy Spirit is leading. (5) Contemplate, be silent and allow the Holy Spirit to transform you.

This process is done slowly and best to be thought of more as yeast for the soul than as a microwave for a quick fix.

Below is a list of reflective questions. Look deep within yourself and ask the Holy Spirit to inspire, direct, and heal you. Ask Him how this Scripture applies to your life. Answer each question completely and honestly. Write down your observations and insights. These reflections will use Scripture in the manner of Lectio Divina, or Divine Reading. Take your time do not rush it through. Use a separate sheet of paper to write your reflections.

Considerations on Self-Discovery

These themes will be included in the Lectio Divina prayer. Most people believe that they are unworthy persons. They often feel inadequate and not worthwhile.

They often try to lead a life that looks normal to the outsider while interiorly, they are in terrible conflict. Most people believe that no one would love them as they are. They have a fear of abandonment and become very isolated from those around them and often push people away. Most people believe that their needs are never going to be met if they have to depend on others. The resulting rage becomes internalized as depression, resentment and self-pity.

We will use these Scriptures for the meditations.

Jesus Forgives and Heals a Paralyzed Man

A few days later, when Jesus again entered Capernaum, the people heard that he had come home. They gathered in such large numbers that there was no room left, not even outside the door, and he preached the word to them. Some men came, bringing to him a paralyzed man, carried by four of them. Since they could not get him to Jesus because of the crowd, they made an opening in the roof above Jesus by digging through it and then lowered the mat the man was lying on. When Jesus saw their faith, he said to the paralyzed man, "Son, your sins are forgiven." Now some teachers of the law were sitting there, thinking to themselves, "Why does this fellow talk like that? He's blaspheming! Who can forgive sins but God alone?"

Immediately Jesus knew in his spirit that this was what they were thinking in their hearts, and he said to them, "Why are you thinking these things? Which is easier: to say to this paralyzed man, 'Your sins are forgiven,' or to say, 'Get up, take your mat and walk'? But I want you to know that the Son of Man has authority on earth to forgive sins." So he said to the man, "I tell you, get up, take your mat and go home." He got up, took his mat and walked out in full view of them all. This amazed everyone and they praised God, saying, "We have never seen anything like this!" (Mark 2:1–12, NIV)

Week 1

Scripture: "Some men came, bring to him a paralyzed man."

Who am I and what paralyzes me?

My family of origin taught me that I am not a worthwhile person. I feel inadequate and a failure. I believe that something is essentially wrong with me. I often feel shame and guilt. These feelings do not go away. I believe that I do not deserve to have good things happen to me. Actually, bad things should happen to me.

I feel unloved and unlovable. My needs will never be met. Consequently, I internalize my rage, and it shows up as depression, resentment, self-pity and even suicidal feelings.

Week 2

Scripture: "Carried by four of them."

How do I relate to my closest friends and family?

I often create a front of normality to hide my inadequacy. I wear a mask all the time. It takes a lot of energy from me. I may even appear to be grandiose and full of exaggerated self-importance, or I pretend to be humble. My real friends and family see that I am conflicted between who I feel that I am and who I pretend to be. They see my decisions or behaviors as irrational and self-destructive.

I assume responsibility for all the pain of loved ones.

I feel isolated. I am often unaware of other peoples' pain or appreciate their opinions.

I cannot depend on others to love me. I do not have confidence in others' love. I expect rejection.

Week 3

Scripture: "Since they could not get him to Jesus because of the crowd, they made an opening in the roof above Jesus by digging through it."

How do others relate to me?

Close friends and family become angry and frustrated with me because of my egocentricities, especially when I am insensitive to others. They are troubled by what looks like destructive or curious behaviors.

I often do extreme or indulgent things as if making up for something.

Significant persons feel pushed away, useless, neglected, and unnecessary. They are confused, seemingly generous gestures, but lack any personal warmth or presence. People become angry and hurt with a sense of abandonment in reaction to my irresponsible behaviors.

Those closest to me see a double life. My ups and downs are difficult to understand. They begin to distrust me. There are inconsistencies between my private and public life.

Week 4

Scripture: "And then lowered the mat the man was lying on."

What embarrasses me, and who would care about me anyway?

I believe that everyone would abandon me if the truth of who I am and what I do would be known. I dare not be dependent on others, reach out to others or let others help me.

I believe that my sexual or other behaviors are so bad that everything becomes my fault.

I believe that something is fundamentally wrong with me. I am embarrassed about who I am and how little I have accomplished. There is no way that I could be good enough.

Week 5

Scripture: "He said to the paralyzed man, 'Your sins are forgiven.'"

Who is Jesus, and how do I relate to him?

If I relate to Jesus at all, it is from a distance. I believe in my head but not my heart.

I sometimes look to Jesus to be my savior, helper, sustainer, but I doubt if He really cares enough about me personally. Hell feels closer to me than heaven.

Jesus could not forgive my sins. There are too many and too big.

Although I speak all the right words about Jesus and my relationship with Him, I do not really trust Him. I avoid His lordship over my life. I have to be in charge of my life.

God the Father and the Holy Spirit are intellectual concepts, not realities that dynamically affect my life.

Week 6

Scripture: "I want you to know that the Son of Man has authority on earth to forgive sins."

What are my sins, and which make me feel the most shame?

I fear that I may be emotional and generally out of control. I often promise to be in better control of myself, but it does not work.

My obsessions pervade my life and behavior. I cover up and lie about who I really am.

I am ashamed of myself

Week 7

Scripture: "Now, some teachers of the law were sitting there, thinking to themselves, 'Why does this fellow talk like that? He's blaspheming!' "

How am I a hypocrite?

I cannot honestly express guilt and remorse because that would require me to be honest with myself, others, and God.

I create a false image of being in charge of my life. I am a perfectionist. I appear to be unaffected by any problem.

I put on the mask of being charming and sociable, but I am really trying to be unreachable and emotionally closed off from others. I appear not to want anything.

I am purposely unclear about my intentions in relationships.

I put a great deal of effort to show that I am respectable and law abiding.

Week 8

Scripture: "Who can forgive sins but God alone?"

How do I try to manipulate others to go along with my beliefs?

I can be calculating, strategizing, manipulative and even ruthless. Rules and laws are made for people who are lovable. Those who are unlovable survive in other ways. I often mislead or lie to people. I will tell them what they want to hear.

My plan for acceptance from others is to be good enough although I know that I am not. Being good enough often means doing things for others that I do not want to. I have a difficult time saying no.

Week 9

Scripture: "Immediately Jesus knew in his spirit that this was what they were thinking in their hearts, and he said to them, 'Why are you thinking these things?'"

What secrets does Jesus know about me that I wish He did not know?

I know that Jesus knows everything about me and that scares me. Although I speak otherwise, I know that I am doomed for sure. Perhaps I can successfully hide from Jesus also.

Week 10

Scripture: "'I want you to know that the Son of Man has authority on earth to forgive sins.' So he said to the man, 'I tell you, get up, take your mat and go home.' He got up, took his mat and walked out in full view of them all."

What sins or emotional problems hold me back from becoming a full and complete person?

I am afraid to trust. No one, even the Divine, is trustworthy. My whole life has validated this. I know this to be true. I am wired not to believe. I often want to believe. Honestly, I am riding on the faith of others and what I read. Although again, being honest, I do not read much. Certainly, I do not read Scripture much or go to church much or even pray much. If I give five minutes a day to God, He is lucky. My laziness and lame excuses of being so busy are really evidence that I do not believe that Jesus is close to me, cares about me, and can affect me in a positive way. Let's be honest, I am more about myself than Jesus.

Week 11

Scripture: "Son, your sins are forgiven."

Who does Jesus say that I am?

I really do not know who I am in Jesus. I know what others have said, but I have not integrated that into myself. Others have said that we are all dirty, rotten sinners but that Jesus can make us good and holy. I believe the dirty rotten part, but the other seems too good

to be true. I do not trust it. I might say the churchy words, but I really do not believe it.

Certainly Jesus would never call me son or daughter.

Week 12

Scripture: "This amazed everyone and they praised God, saying, 'We have never seen anything like this!'"

What amazing things would you like God to do for you?

- CHAPTER 18 -
RULE OF LIFE

If you do not have a Rule of Life, life will rule you.

Sometimes it seems that life rules your work, family, God, prayer and church. St. Benedict wrote his Holy Rule "so that, you may return to Him from whom you had departed by the sloth of disobedience... Come my children listen to me; I will teach you the fear of the Lord. Run while you have the light of life, lest the darkness of death overtake you... And so we are going to establish a school for the service of the Lord."

I have always believed that original sin was essentially motivated by pride but energized by sloth. Both pride and sloth are certainly entertaining us today.

If you have heard and responded to the Word of God and said, "Here I am, Lord," and seek to be on the mountain with the Lord of all Life, the Holy Rule of St. Benedict teaches, as a school, how to be with Him and simultaneously live in the world. The Holy Rule is for everyone who wants to listen with the ear of your heart. It can be applied to every walk of life. It is down-to-earth, realistic, and compassionate.

The Rule of St. Benedict, Conversion, Stability, Obedience

The Rule of St. Benedict has influenced the Church throughout the centuries. What is most impressive about the Holy Rule of St. Benedict is the fact that it has been with us for 1,500 years and is still relevant and contemporary. Throughout the centuries, it was adopted as a Rule of Life by numberless male and female monastics, religious orders, autonomous monasteries, religious families and congregations, lay oblates and lay associations. The Rule transcends factions, divisions, denominations, rites, politics and administrative red tape. One can find monastics, religious and lay people living the Rule of St. Benedict alike in all Christian faith expressions.

The Rule of St. Benedict is ecumenical. It covers all the practical aspects of life and is valued as a guide to a simple life lived fully in homes, businesses, churches, as well as monasteries. It leads those living under the Rule toward a holy life and to encounter God face-to-face and to create a personal experience with God.

You might think of religious vows as "dead man walking." Your life as you know it is over. No more smiles, no more friends, no more fun. Actually, religious vows are a vehicle to more freedom. The Rule of St. Benedict is a guide and the kind of life that Christians want to celebrate. They want a simple life, lived well. The last place that a Christian seeks is the whirlwind of earthbound stress, confusion, fear and fragility.

Following a Rule of Life provides direction on healthy choices rather than making decisions forced upon us by fearful stress. The Rule of St. Benedict is a time honored way of life that provides guidance on life's challenges. Conversatio, or conversion of heart, is not referring to one's initial conversion into Christianity. Rather the daily desire to grow and change beyond our current earthbound paradigms. Those changes can be challenging, but having a Rule of Life and other like-minded persons helping you, the pilgrimage becomes rather liberating and exciting. Life begins to become simple.

Stability is seeking God within the Cistercian community. It does not mean giving up your church, family, employment and other responsibilities. The Cistercian community becomes a complementary asset.

We think of ourselves as extended family. We dedicate ourselves to God the Father, God the Son and God the Holy Spirit and in all things trusting in the power of grace and in the love and support of the brothers in this community.

Obedience is the most liberating of all. It means being able to trust and gain your confidence under the direction of a loving compassionate leader. You will never be asked to do the impossible or anything that is outside of the Cistercian governing documents that include Scripture. Now your simple life is lived well.

Benedictine/Cistercian Spirituality
What is Benedictine Spirituality?

Benedictine Spirituality is a way of life in which one follows Christ in the footsteps of St. Benedict as prescribed in his Holy Rule. We also follow our Constitution and the Manual of the Cistercian Order of the Holy Cross.

Benedictine Spirituality is practical and profound. The Rule of St. Benedict has often been referred to as a compendium of the Holy Gospel of Jesus Christ.

The Throne of God

Benedictine/Cistercian monasteries are palaces where the glory of God shines out. Monks are called to seek and abide in the love of God through the celebration of the Eucharistic Liturgy and the singing and reciting of the Office.

Humility is fundamental to monastic life. Humility makes our communities the throne of God. St. Benedict invites us to build a community in which we are liberated from rivalry, competition and power struggles. This implies a profound challenge to the modern cult of self.

The Cistercians, a reformed Benedictine movement to which we belong, developed a profound spirituality based on solid theological anthropology such as knowledge of self in community, love and mystical contemplation.

Indeed the Rule offers each person a direct path to Gospel perfection through a careful balance between the traditional monastic observance and our contemporary culture. Catholics and Protestants alike have benefited from the teachings of St. Benedict.

Benedictine/Cistercian Spirituality
General Overview

- Preferring nothing to the love of Christ
- Joyfully accepting the blessing of obedience, practicing fraternal charity, progressing in the conversion of life and the practice of humility
- Greater places of silence, peace, brotherhood and ecumenical sensitivity
- Authentic religious perfection
- Witnesses of the theological virtue of hope
- The experience of God and the Benedictine approach to prayer
- The search for God
- *Obsculta*, "listen with the ears of your heart." We listen, trusting that God is there and that God will speak
- Burning passion for God, discipline and discipleship
- Spirit of hospitality
- The luminous figure of St. Benedict stands in our midst, pointing always to Christ

- Contemplative silence
- Devotion to Mary to whom the Cistercian Order is consecrated
- Faithfulness to our way of life as we live in charity and courage

Benedictine Spirituality

Benedictine/Cistercian Spirituality is not a spirituality of escape. It is a spirituality that fills time and space with an awareness of the presence of God. For this purpose, Benedict called for prayer at regular intervals of each day. Benedictine prayer has several characteristics that make it more of a spirituality of awareness than of consolation. It is regular, converting, reflective and communal. Out of these qualities, a whole new life emerges and people are changed.

We pray to see life as God sees it, to understand it and to make it better. We pray to dispose ourselves to God, "Here I am, Lord." We pray to open our hearts and minds to be challenged and changed by God and our neighbors. From this is born the Benedictine or Cistercian monastic vows of obedience, stability and conversion. For the true contemplative, all is God, all is prayer.

Benedictine Spirituality Is Humane

St. Benedict knew that the regeneration of the individual generally is not to be reached by the path of solitude, nor by that of austerity, but by the beaten path of man's social instinct, with its necessary conditions of obedience and work and that neither the body nor the mind can be safely overstrained in the effort to avoid evil.

Ora et Labora, Opus Dei, silence, solitude, simplicity material, and spiritual simplicity, work, prayer and study are a must for cultivating a contemplative atmosphere, both within and around. The result should be *Pax* (Peace).

Monastic Silence at the Service of Prayer

Silence or restraint of speech operates at many levels and is an act of discipline proper to the spiritual art. It necessitates that state of tranquility which makes possible greater attention to the non-sensate realities of the spiritual world. Different levels and degrees of monastic/spiritual silence are as follows:

- Reduction of Physical Noise
- Avoidance of the Sins of the Tongue
- Conservation of Energy
- Attentive Listening
- Concentration
- Listening with the Heart

The only way to pray is to pray, and the way to pray well is to pray much. If one has no time for this, then one must at least pray regularly. But the less one prays, the worse prayer gets.

When one has imbued oneself in prayer, silence, and solitude, it becomes almost impossible to believe that life's journey ends at the grave. Following Christ under a Rule and an Abbot, community life becomes a school of the Lord's service and a training ground for brotherly love.

The Cistercian Order of the Holy Cross, Common Observance

We, the Cistercians of the Holy Cross, are embedded icons, living sacramentals; who sustain, grace and hold together the fiber of our communities.

We live in and are influenced by the heretic nature of our culture. However, while clothed in our holy habits, we become sacred icons.

When people gaze upon us, they look into their hope and see reflected back the Source of all hope. We become sacred signs, living sacramentals.

The Pax of our contemplative lives provides the necessary stillness to speak without words.

The Cistercian Order of the Holy Cross, Common Observance, is an independent dispersed religious order within the One, Holy, Catholic and Apostolic Church and an autonomous member of the Independent Anglican Church, Canada Synod.

We describe ourselves as living under a Common Observance because our Order allows for much flexibility in exercising the Cistercian charism. We also try to be open to the authentic movement of the Holy Spirit in our time and place.

Some unique aspects of the Order of the Holy Cross are:

- First order monks are single or married. Our members live in their homes and continue their usual family, work and church responsibilities.
- They may perform works of charity, pastoral ministry and mission work. Priests and deacons of or in the Order may be single or married. We have a realistic formation program for those men who wish to be ordained.

147

- Men and women from both the Historic and Protestant churches may participate as third order oblates.

Our typical members are single or married working men and women who are active in their church and community and desire to advance in their intimate relationship with God. Several of our members are advanced in age and have a physical disability.

In brief

We serve men and women, clerical or lay, married or single by:

- Helping them grow in perfection through the use of the Rule of St. Benedict, our Constitution, the Manual, and community life.
- Consecrating to a first-order religious life those who desire such a commitment.
- Validating and assisting those already living the religious life but not living in a formal community.
- Helping those who desire a lesser involvement in a monastic life through our third-order oblate program.
- Supporting men with a call to priesthood through ordination, incardination or encouraging those who wish to stay in their existing jurisdictions.
- Encouraging our membership in a contemplative life as well as in works of charity, pastoral ministry and mission work.

Please read our website CistercianMonks.org. If you have any questions or would like to apply, feel free to write me personally:

The Rt. Rev. Oscar Joseph, OCCO
Abbot General
Holy Cross Monastery
1606 Briar Lake Circle
Winston-Salem, NC 27103-6647
Abbot@Bellsouth.net

ABOUT THE AUTHOR

The Right Reverend Oscar Joseph, O.C.C.O. holds a Master's of Science in Education, doctoral degrees in Sacred Theology (Scripture) and Christian Counseling, as well as several honorary doctorates.

He has been a TV and radio personality, former pastor of a local conservative Anglican Church, college educator, retreat master and seminar leader.

Ordained a priest in 1993, Abbot Oscar Joseph is currently a Bishop in the Independent Anglican Church, Canada Synod and serves as the Abbot General of the Cistercian Order of the Holy Cross. The Cistercian Order is a contemplative worldwide religious Order and one of the oldest of its type. Abbot Oscar Joseph has been called a leader in the Benedictine movement in the United States.

Abbot Oscar Joseph has been a Christian Counselor and Spiritual Director to hundreds over the past thirty-five years. He has authored a number of books, including

Memoirs of a Christian Healer, The Joy of Spiritual Freedom, (with his wife, Kathleen Rivest PhD, DD), along with numerous articles on spiritual direction, ˉliturgy, emotional fitness and leisure. He has also conducted healing services throughout the East Coast of the United States. Abbot Oscar Joseph was the founder and principal counselor at the St. Matthew's Institute from 1987 to 2019.

Abbot Oscar Joseph has an extensive background as an educator. He taught psychology, sociology, Old and New Testament, English and ethics at several local community colleges. He is the Founder/President of St. Stephen Harding Theological College and Seminary, which provides a scholarly and classically Anglo-Catholic educational experience.

Retired from his counseling practice in 2019, Abbot Oscar Joseph is currently focused on his duties as leader of the Cistercian Order, providing spiritual direction, conducting seminars and healing services.

If you are interested in having Abbot Oscar Joseph OCCO conduct seminars, healing services or wish information on the Cistercian Order, he may be contacted at Abbot@bellsouth.net. More information can be found at Cistercian Order of the Holy Cross (CistercianMonks.org) and St. Stephen Harding Theological College and Seminary (StephenHarding.College).